Praise for *There Is an I in Team*

"I've long held the philosophy that to best educate we must first entertain. Mark de Rond achieves exactly this through his insightful, well researched, and witty look at high performance through the eyes of sport."

—John Eales, Rugby World Cup–winning
captain and businessman

"Mark elucidates what anyone who sits on a sports team or manages a business knows in their gut to be true—talented individuals matter. His value is in moving beyond this simple statement and showing, through anecdote and evidence, how to actually benefit from this knowledge."

—Kip McDaniel,
Editor-in-Chief, *aiCIO*

"As a sportsman, my significant gains often came when challenging and being challenged by the competitive nature of my teammates. As a businessman, I have spent a couple of decades modeling my coach. The best leaders have the ability to create a performance environment where talent can thrive. In this book, Mark has shown how to do this and gone straight to the heart of my world and my identity."

—Adrian Moorhouse, Managing Director, Lane4
Consulting, and Olympic Gold Medalist, Swimming

THERE IS AN I IN TEAM

THERE IS AN I IN TEAM

What Elite Athletes and Coaches Really Know About High Performance

MARK DE ROND

Harvard Business Review Press

Boston, Massachusetts

10 9 8 7 6 5 4 3 2 1

No part of this publication may be reproduced, stored in or introduced into a retrieval system, or transmitted, in any form, or by any means (electronic, mechanical, photocopying, recording, or otherwise), without the prior permission of the publisher. Requests for permission should be directed to permissions@hbsp.harvard.edu, or mailed to Permissions, Harvard Business School Publishing, 60 Harvard Way, Boston, Massachusetts 02163.

Library of Congress Cataloging-in-Publication Data

Rond, Mark de.
    There is an I in team : what elite athletes and coaches really know about high performance / Mark de Rond.
        p. cm.
    ISBN 978-1-4221-7130-1 (alk. paper)
    1. Teams in the workplace. 2. Teamwork (Sports) 3. Performance. I. Title.
    HD66.R648 2012
    658.4'022—dc23

                                                                2012003196

The paper used in this publication meets the requirements of the American National Standard for Permanence of Paper for Publications and Documents in Libraries and Archives Z39.48-1992.

There may not be an I in Team . . .

but there is in Win.

—MICHAEL JORDAN

For Roxana
(Who else?)

Contents

Foreword

Brimming with insight for anyone privileged to lead or work as a member of a team in business, this book sheds new light on the inherent conflict between the team and the individuals comprising the team—there *is* an *I* in team—and explores the profound implications of this simple idea for managing team performance.

There Is an I in Team is not for the faint-hearted. It debunks many of the long-held assumptions that we've built into our development of teams and performance, and outlines a set of guiding principles for how to approach team performance differently.

I first encountered Mark de Rond's work when I heard him give an inspiring talk on the subject of team leadership to partners at a prestigious law firm. Mark was sharing some of his latest findings on team performance from his recent study of the Cambridge University Boat Club.

What could his lengthy and intimate study of one of the oldest sporting events in the world—the annual Boat Race between Cambridge and Oxford on the River Thames—possibly suggest to people in all probability more driven by billable hours than by the time it might take a couple of Blue Boats to get down the Thames?

I had particular reason for paying close attention. I failed my trial as a St. John's College coxswain in 1978 despite, at the time, weighing in at a mere 8 stone (112 lbs.). Mark would surely offer clues as to where I had gone wrong.

I observed the teams of lawyers as Mark mesmerized and challenged them: How much confidence did they have in their own judgment versus that of their colleagues? Did they think it was more important to be competent or likable? Why might emotion and intuition trump analysis and reason, even with teams of lawyers?

Even the most rational in the room were persuaded by Mark's insights from the world of sports showing that significant improvement in performance could be catalyzed by a better understanding—and management—of the inherent tensions between the individuals and the team.

The Boat Race study, and other studies that Mark has undertaken among scientists, engineers, and comedians, for example, equips him with abundant wisdom on the subject of individual and team performance. His credibility, conviction, and inspiration, in my view, can largely be attributed to his research method. Very similar to the Xploring research we use for Saatchi & Saatchi's clients, it is based on the simple idea that, if you want to know how a tiger hunts, you don't go to the zoo, you go to the jungle.

Mark's enlightening, ethnographic exploration into teams and how they perform has led him to live—literally—with diverse teams in extraordinary contexts, like the Cambridge University Boat Club preparing for the annual race down the Thames and, most recently, in Helmand province with a team of military surgeons. He has no predetermined discussion guideline, no series of set questions, no idea, in fact, where his exploration will lead. He merely takes with him an intense curiosity and a willingness to get involved. Combined with knowledge of the latest research on teams in organizations that you'd expect from a Cambridge business school professor, the result of Mark's close-up observation is a volume of actionable learning, steeped in stories and rich in revelation.

At Saatchi & Saatchi, a purpose-inspired creative company, the ideas in this book are especially relevant. We employ highly creative people and need them to be able to perform at their individual peak, while at the same time embracing our team values and collective aspiration—to help our clients fill the world with "Lovemarks" (Saatchi & Saatchi's term for those brands that earn "Loyalty Beyond Reason"). Guided by a theory of peak performance championed by our chief executive, Kevin Roberts, we have used the ideas in *There Is an I in Team* to reconcile the tension between the *I* and the *We* in our daily activity.

For example, without some very clear articulation of an inspirational dream, a shared set of beliefs, and a daily focus (an answer to what Mark calls "The Stephens Question"), our diverse collection of creative talent might well wreak havoc on the organization: we do, after all, invite our people relentlessly to pursue world-changing ideas, and we encourage them to embrace our belief in the unreasonable power of creativity.

So there is plenty of express permission given to the *I*'s in our teams and the unreasonable behavior that our ambition demands.

Significantly, however, we also choose to preface our famous spirit, "Nothing is Impossible," arguably the greatest alibi for the *I,* with the words, "One Team, One Dream."

The inherent paradox between the two phrases is no accident, and we have used the ideas in this book to manage and profit from it. What matters to individuals, Mark argues, is something to care about more than themselves, what we at Saatchi & Saatchi call a lovable purpose. What also matters is an environment in which the *I* can flourish; without it people may still understand the greater purpose, but they can, and will, choose to withhold their discretionary effort.

In our competitive industry, we would simply not be able to transform our clients' businesses without the brilliance of those flawed creative people—all those magnificent *I*'s—riddled with insecurity and resistant to being overtly led, and not always performing at their best on the team.

There Is an I in Team gives us a new and invaluable body of inspiration with which to further excite our people to live the Saatchi & Saatchi purpose, as well as to help them create and articulate their own personal purpose.

As to my own abject failure to win that place as a college coxswain, I now realize why those making the selection had impeccable judgment on that occasion.

The likability card that I played (as you will see, one of the book's key insights is that a person's likability can trump competence in his effect on team performance) was wholly insufficient to mask an extraordinary incompetence in the cox's seat. There is no place for that on any team.

—Richard Hytner
Saatchi & Saatchi

Preface

This book is about talented individuals and the challenge of fashioning them into a high-performance team. Chances are that you know what I am alluding to: however brilliant and well intended your colleagues may be, natural team players they are not. Yet teamwork is imperative to their success, and to yours, too.

This book tackles the leadership challenges of harnessing and then optimizing the influence of individuals on teams. It is written for the kinds of people I teach: clever, purposeful, tenacious, inquisitive. Despite good intentions, they can find it difficult to make teams add up to more than the sum of their parts. They work hard and expect others to follow suit. They routinely compare themselves to their peers and suspect this is reciprocal. They are hungry for feedback. They are busy. Their need for achievement has become an addiction. Many were part of successful teams in the past but struggle to achieve that same level of performance with their current peers. Their underlying questions are always the same: Why isn't my team performing to its potential? Given our pool of experience, talent, and ambition, why are things not what they could be? How can I get talented people to work together more successfully?

This book will offer some answers to these questions. But they are not the typical answers contained in other business books. For one, it looks at teams through the lens of sports. Through first-hand accounts of elite athletes, elite teams, and their coaches, it develops a deeper, grittier, real-world understanding of high performance in teams than is commonplace. It augments their experiences with the very best scholarship in social psychology, organizational behavior, and the economics and sociology of sports, extracted from the desks, classrooms, and experimental labs of the world's top universities: Harvard, Cambridge, Stanford, Berkeley, and Chicago, among others. For despite an abundance of books on sports and business, few have drawn explicit comparisons between the two. Fewer yet have done so with the rigor expected by today's professional, which is somewhat surprising insofar as sports and business have long been bedfellows.

A recent survey of a hundred randomly selected CEOs of the United Kingdom's five hundred largest companies found that 46 percent of the CEOS had won awards for their athletic prowess (by comparison, only 23 percent had accumulated awards for academic achievement). Seventy-one percent believed that compulsory sports at school shaped their business acumen in a positive way.[1] Scott McNealy, Jack Welch, Vera Wang, Meg Whitman, and Phil Knight have all publicly acknowledged their debt to sports as vital to their commercial success.[2] Real estate magnate Thomas Barrack Jr. never realized his ambitions to play football for the University of Southern California, and was relegated to playing rugby instead. Film, television, and stage actor Hill Harper dreamed of playing for the Dallas Cowboys or San Francisco 49ers, only to be told, during his college years, that he wasn't big enough. Fashion designer Richie Rich never made it to the Olympics as a figure skater; neither did Vera Wang. Marcus Samuelsson succeeded as chef and restaurateur but failed as a soccer player. Editor-in-chief Lucy Danziger was too short to make crew. Donny Deutsch, chairman of Deutsch Inc., never got beyond Little League baseball. NBC's president and CEO Jeff Zucker never made it to Wimbledon; Nike's Phil Knight was never on the Olympic running track team. Without fail, all of them hated the experience of finding themselves at the short end of the stick, whether through injury or lack of ability.[3] All hung on to the lessons they picked up in their sporting days to help them make good commercially.

This book will dip into the experiences of some of them, as well as into the stories of elite athletes and coaches such as Michael Jordan, Phil Jackson, Magic Johnson, Bobby Fischer, Joe DiMaggio, Bill Hartack, Billy Beane, Bill Walsh, Pete Carroll, Eric Cantona, Zinédine Zidane, John Eales, David Whitaker, Sir Alex Ferguson, Adrian Moorhouse, Seve Ballesteros, and Brian Clough. Their experiences challenge commonplace ideas about teams and provide fresh insights into high performance.

Also, this book focuses unashamedly on the individual in the context of other individuals. Much popular business writing on teams risks missing the trees for the forest and, in doing so, masks genuine insights that sporting teams offer their counterparts in the workplace. Pick up almost any popular business book or article on teams written over the past two decades. Their principal unit of analysis has often been the team (the forest), and not the individual (the tree) in the context of other high performers. They focus on what matters to the organization, assuming the organization matters to individuals. With few exceptions, you will find their authors emphasizing the importance of interpersonal harmony, having assumed this to be a stimulant to team performance rather than its consequence. They have often focused exclusively on the importance of cooperation without considering the relevance of competition within teams. They looked to recruiting stars from outside instead of growing theirs in-house. Their interest has become focused on statistics at the expense of intuition, and on the import of change rather than stability. This book seeks to correct all that.

My concern with trees and forests stems from my academic fieldwork. For the past fifteen years, this has involved studying teams close up, in many cases by living with them for extended periods for up to two hundred consecutive days (and nights) at a time.[4] I began my research while a doctoral student at the University of Oxford in 1996 with a three-year study of life scientists in pursuit of new medicinal drugs. Next up was a study of engineers collaborating in virtual teams at one of the world's largest telecommunications companies, a collaboration with a colleague from MIT. We're both still a little self-conscious about never having produced a single piece of writing on what amounted to a good two years of study. But both the engineers and a subsequent team of improvisation comedians bear on the arguments in this book. So too do observations from an ongoing study of military surgeons, begun in early 2009, and culminating in six weeks of predeployment training followed by a six-week "tour of duty" in Afghanistan's Helmand province. Nothing comes close to the experience of watching surgical teams at work in the world's busiest, and bloodiest, war hospital. Camp Bastion's fifty-bed hospital uses more blood than all of Scotland combined. It also has the highest survival rate of any war hospital in any previous war.

More germane to this particular volume, however, is a two-year study of the Cambridge University Boat Club squad as it prepared to race Oxford rivals in the quintessential Boat Race, first rowed in 1829 and followed by an estimated 120 million around the world via their television screens. The squad's trials and tribulations were the subject of another book, *The Last Amateurs: To Hell and Back with the Cambridge Boat Race Crew.* Controversial but extraordinarily candid, it was enjoyed not only by sports enthusiasts but by those struggling with their workplace teams. Bits of the research appeared in *The Economist, Time,* the *Financial Times, Forbes, Harvard Business Review, The Week,* most of Britain's national broadsheets, and on *BBC* radio. Drawing from that book, I reproduce here some of the most inspiring of the squad's experiences along with unpublished interviews and analyses. Their stories, along with those of Olympic gold medalists and World Champions, are included for one reason only, namely to provide a genuinely close-up, visceral experience of the graphic and uncompromising reality that characterizes everyday life in teams of high performers.

This book develops some of the themes buried deeply (too deeply perhaps) in what my Cambridge colleagues teasingly refer to as "the rowing book." In contrast to *The Last Amateurs,* this book is deeply embedded in scholarship, and in combining cutting-edge research with firsthand accounts of top athletes, coaches, and corporate executives, it explains:

- Why there *is* an I in team—and why that matters

- Why the best team rarely ever comprises the best individual performers

- Why conflict happens even as intentions are perfectly aligned

- Why likability can trump competence in even technically sophisticated environments

- Why a focus on interpersonal harmony can actually hurt team performance

- Why the availability of data and sophisticated statistical tools are unlikely to ever eradicate the role of intuition

These are but a few themes lifted from the chapters that make up this book. Each chapter is intended to tease out a particular feature of teams—usually a commonly held, but false, belief—and then show the evidence, from the world of sports, for a better, alternative way to think about elite individuals and team performance.

As for the use of examples, each chapter typically invokes some high-profile athletes, before broadening the illustrations to sports and teams that are less well known, but not any less instructive. North American readers will be less familiar with the examples from soccer, rugby, and field hockey. But they'll be acquainted with the likes of Michael Jordan, Phil Jackson, Pete Reiser, and Bobby Fischer. For the rest of the world, the less familiar examples might include football, baseball, basketball, and ice hockey. Their acquaintance is with such stars as Zinédine Zidane, John Eales, and Adrian Moorhouse. Beyond these examples, each chapter also includes one in-depth piece of analysis from my own ethnographic work.

My greatest worry in writing this book was always that sports might seem a spent metaphor. After all, sporting metaphors are now such a conspicuous feature of the management vernacular. We "level the playing field" by "sending in heavy hitters" who happily "step up to the plate" and will "take one for the team." We "keep our eyes on the ball," aim for the "sweet spot," "take a free throw," or perhaps a "Hail Mary pass," while reckoning "there's still time on the clock" and "the goalposts have moved." Meanwhile we are told "there's no I in team" or else we're "shown the red card" in what seems like "a new ballgame" where "the odds" of "a knockout blow" are more likely to make us feel like "an outsider" than "a good sport." We tell "young guns" to "make a pitch" and "go for gold" or else "throw in the towel" at "the final stretch."

Ronald Reagan spoke of the "World Series of tax reform," while President Obama's White House press secretary Robert Gibbs had this to say about progress of the economic stimulus bill: "Bottom of the fifth [inning], the sausage race is [at] the beginning of the next inning, so stay tuned, and the starting pitcher is in there, still throwing nice curveballs and [he's] still got a lot of heat on the fastball."[5] He also spoke of the American war effort as needing to "defend this country on the extremists' 10-yard line, and not on our 10-yard line."[6] Though sports metaphors permeate business parlance, my goal in this book is to offer managers and anyone on a team in business some real, substantive ideas about how to be a better player—or manager—based on what we know from the world of elite sports.

Acknowledgments

In writing this book, I benefited greatly from the generosity of CEOs, senior executives, and sports coaches, from Olympic medalists, World Champions, and from those who never reached their athletic ambitions but went on to do other things instead. Prominent among them are Lane4's Matt Rogan, Adrian Moorhouse, Austin Swain, and Kerry Walsh. Richard Hytner, deputy chairman of Saatchi & Saatchi Worldwide, wrote the foreword. One of the world's most successful advertising firms, its success hinges critically on getting teams of brilliant but strong-minded individuals to work together.

For detailed insights into workplace teams, I am particularly grateful to KPMG's Steve Hollis, former Herbert Smith senior partner Tim Bellis, ex-McKinsey partner Steve Hacking, Cobra Beer's Lord Karan Bilimoria, and former managing director of Dixons, Nick Wilkinson, as well as anonymous contributions from individuals at McLaren, IBM, McKinsey, Slaughter and May, PricewaterhouseCoopers, OfCom, KPMG, Xchanging, Taylor Vintners, Underwriters Laboratories, Herbert Smith, Stephenson Harwood, Addleshaw Goddard, Lloyds-TSB, Diageo, Rolls-Royce, Bank of China, British Telecom, and many others.

In sports, my sources include lengthy discussions with John Eales, David Hemery, Matt Guinness King, Adrian Moorhouse, Austin Swain, Mark Richardson, Graham Smith, Wil James, Duncan Holland, Jake Cornelius, Kieran West, Tom James, and Brendan Purcell. I benefited greatly from the generosity of Duncan Holland, Rob Baker, and Grant Craies in allowing me to study their coaching practices up close for two years, and from conversations with Chris Nilsson (who produced a stunningly effective albeit unhappy Cambridge crew) and Steve Trapmore (an Olympic gold medalist and current head coach of CUBC).

Much good came of doing what academics do best: to trail through thick stacks of biographies as well as first-person accounts of life in sports. I received helpful editorial support from Chris Dalley, Kip McDaniel, Matt Rogan, Andreas Richter, Daniel Siekhaus, Richard Hackman, Conrad Chua, Peter Mahoney, Mark Midwinter, Anthony Lambert, Adam Brooks, my students in Cambridge, and my editor Melinda Merino. She is everything anyone could ever ask for editorially, as well as a brilliant source of good ideas. This book is far better for her engagement. Whatever imperfections remain are, as usual, my fault.

1

Why There Is
an *I* in Team

The Old:	There is no *I* in team.
The New:	There is an *I* in team. And it matters.
The Challenge:	To exploit individual qualities while mitigating the risks these same qualities entail.

Good spelling does not equal deep thinking. Take that old devil, "there is no *I* in team." When basketball star Michael Jordan, after a run of twenty straight points, snubbed Coach Tex Winter with, "there may not be an *I* in team, but there is in win," he may have been onto something. A basketball team without superstars rarely makes it to the playoffs, let alone the finals. Such star players as Magic Johnson, Larry Bird, Michael Jordan, Kobe Bryant, Tim Duncan, Shaquille O'Neal, Hakeem Olajuwon, and LeBron James have consistently featured in all but one NBA finals series for the last thirty years. In fact, a team with no starting all-star player has less than a 1/100th chance of winning the championship. By comparison, a team with an all-star player raises the odds of winning to 7.1 percent and of making it to the finals to 16 percent.

These odds increase dramatically as the number of star players per team increases. Those teams with pockets deep enough to field two first-team all-star players have a one-in-four chance of winning a championship and better than a one-in-three chance of making the finals. With three all-stars, these odds increase to 39 percent and 77 percent, respectively. And the argument holds even when controlling for a team's winning percentage during the regular season. When it comes to the playoffs, a star player improves his or her team's chances of winning a championship by 12 percent. A superstar with a relatively weak supporting cast fares better than a team with five good players.[1] Love them or loathe them, individuals matter.

So much then for that old devil. While grammatically correct, as a guiding principle, it is flawed and impractical. It downplays the extent to which high-performance teams benefit from variations in talent, in personality, and even in pay. And it diminishes the value of competition between team members. Even those blissful moments of team flow, when mind and matter fuse effortlessly as all are absorbed in the task at hand are more often than not the consequence of individual differences cleverly brought into play by good leadership. The choice of who is in and who is not will have been decided based on the relevance of particularized attributes to an available set of competencies. In sports as in business, it is the *combination* that matters. Even in teams that are greatly interdependent and prize uniformity—think of synchronized swimming or team sprints in cycling—individuality can be a positive differentiator. Besides, no matter how resolute the belief that individuality be completely eradicated, to collaborate effectively remains a matter of personal choice.

Team decisions require individuals to commit to those around them and to be accountable for their own performance to the team. Should they choose to commit, they will only ever do so for their own reasons. As one of Britain's most distinguished coaches, David Whitaker, put it: "If you want an exceptional team, keep your eye on the individual . . . Teams thrive on individual choice and commitment . . . the most powerful teams are made up of individuals who have chosen to work as a team."[2] Having coached hockey teams to Olympic gold and bronze, World and European silver, he deserves to be taken seriously.

Thus, teams begin and end with individuals. This is not an ideological statement. Nor is it a normative one. This book has no intention of lionizing individuals at the expense of teams or of, God forbid, sanctioning egotism. It does not prioritize individual over collective effort (even if some tasks—particularly those that require logical problem solving—are often better done by individuals than teams). It doesn't even go as far as Jordan's gibe. Its perspective is far subtler. To focus on the *I* in teams is to pursue a very specific level of granularity. It is to see the trees for the forest by granting individuals that degree of choice missing in much popular writing on teams. To keep in mind the individual is to emphasize precisely the sorts of issues that are easily lost when considering teams as the primary unit of analysis.

Thus, the chapters in this book explore each of the following assertions: The qualities that make individuals attractive can make them difficult. The best individuals put together do not necessarily make for the most effective team. Conflict often arises even as people agree on what needs to be done and why, and actively try to coordinate their efforts with those around them. Their productivity depends on who else is involved, and how many of them there are. It can make sense to trade off competence for likability within a team in even technically demanding environments. Competition within teams can be as valuable as collaboration.

The *I* in team also suggests that the key to managing teams lies not just in advanced statistical techniques, skill complementarities, or team bonding but in an appreciation of their *humanity*. When teams work well, it is because, and not in spite, of individual differences. These differences are at once a source of brilliance and tension, leaving teams poised between entropy and synergy, tension and collective genius.

What may appear like picture-perfect teams are then in reality often quite intricate tapestries of distinct characters united by a common goal but forced into a sanctum where trade-off choices must be made between likability and competence; where powerful but conflicting pressures coexist; where one's success hinges on being able to reconcile camaraderie and rivalry, trust and vigilance, the sacred and the profane; and where they end up getting it wrong as often as right.

These teams can feel fragile to those on the inside, even if perfectly functional on the outside. In contrast to popular belief, teams of high performers are not easy places to be. At times, they are anything but harmonious, but then harmony may well be the result, not cause, of superior performance. Workplace teams are even more complex. Businesses rarely have the luxury of focusing on a single team with one clear objective. The composition of the *I*'s in charge of production will invariably be different to the composition of the *I*'s in charge of sales or R&D. Adding to this complexity, sitting on top of these various teams is typically a small team (the executives) charged with understanding, leading, and managing the multiplicity of teams in their business. And the *I*'s inside them.

4

What Makes Them Good Makes Them Difficult, Too

This chapter and those that follow will try to untangle the tapestry of high-performance teams to identify the true nature of collective performance. They do so by using insights from elite sports, occasionally supplemented by evidence from experiments in social psychology, organizational behavior, and the sociology and economics of sports. The first of these insights is in some ways also the most exasperating: it seems one cannot have one's cake and eat it too when it comes to turning teams of high performers into high performance teams. With few exceptions, the qualities that make individuals as gifted as they are can make them wearisome as team members. They are often extraordinarily focused, with higher-than-usual thresholds for personal discomfort. This is true in sports as much as in business.

Consider, for example, 1940s baseball star Pete Reiser. Known colloquially as "Pistol Pete," he had to be carried off the diamond eleven times in two and a half years of playing in the minors, three in the army, and ten in the majors (with the Brooklyn Dodgers, Pittsburgh Pirates, Cleveland Indians, and Boston Braves). According to W. C. Heinz's 1958 biopic, "nine times Pete regained consciousness either in the clubhouse or in hospital. He broke a bone in his right elbow, throwing. He broke both ankles, tore a cartilage in his left knee, ripped the muscles in his left leg, sliding. Seven times he crashed into outfield walls, dislocating his left shoulder, breaking his right collarbone and, five times, ending up an unconscious heap on the ground."[3] Yet, according to the *New York Herald Tribune's* Bob Crooke, "Pete Reiser was the best ballplayer I ever saw."[4] Reiser would have it no other way. Nor would we.

In the workplace, personal discomfort is rarely of the same muscular variety, limited instead to sleep deprivation, a poor work-life balance, and excess consumption of food or alcohol or both. But occasionally we find extremes here, too. The managing partner of one of the world's largest and most profitable professional services firms who, realizing that his highly successful team of partners experienced a disproportionally high incidence of divorce, decided to retain the services of one of London's top divorce lawyers. Doing so helped mitigate the anxiety and additional workload generated by this real, even if unintentional, consequence of a ruthless focus at work. The example is brutal but too often true: what seemed good for business proved detrimental to the families implicated by it, usually by no choice of their own.

Insofar as their focus is invariably bound up with a proclivity for perfectionism, here is how Italian soccer manager Carlo Ancelotti describes one of the game's most successful coaches: "He [Fabio Capello] was very serious, meticulous and I don't think there is anybody better than him at reading a game. On a human level, well, that's a different story. He didn't have a dialogue with us, he just told us what to do. And, unsurprisingly, he fell out with many players. For example, I remember Ruud Gullit [voted World Soccer Player of the Year in 1987 and 1989] pinning him up against the wall. The rest of us intervened to break it up, even though, secretly, I think many players were cheering for Ruud."[5]

Within the world of commerce, few better examples exist than the late Steve Jobs. Adored around the world for the elegance and user-friendliness of his designs, Jobs was many things, including selfish, rude, aggressive, paranoid, lachrymose, and unpredictable, at least to those who worked with him.[6] But it is his relentless perfectionism (such as making sure the magnetic laptop charger made just the right sort of click) that we adore him for. As Wired.com's news editor, Leander Kahney, wrote before Jobs's premature death:

Apple creates must-have products the old-fashioned way: by locking the doors and sweating and bleeding until something emerges perfectly formed . . . Jobs is a notorious microman-ager. No product escapes Cupertino without meeting Jobs' exacting standards, which are said to cover such esoteric details as the number of screws on the bottom of a laptop and the curve of a monitor's corners . . . At most companies, the red-faced, tyrannical boss is an outdated archetype, a carica-ture from the life of Dagwood. Not at Apple. Whereas the rest of the tech industry may motivate employees with carrots, Jobs is known as an inveterate stick man. Even the most favored employee could find themselves on the receiving end of a tirade. Insiders have a term for it: the "hero-shithead roller coaster." Jeffrey Bewkes, CEO of Time Warner, found him unvarnished and prone to using colorful language.[7] Says Edward Eigerman, a former Apple engineer, "More than any-where else I've worked before or since, there's a lot of concern about being fired." . . . A Silicon Valley insider once [said] he had seen Jobs demean many people and make some of them cry. But, the insider added, "He was almost always right."[8]

Couldn't work with him. Wouldn't want a world without him. But do perfectionism, paranoia, tenacity, and self-confidence really make individuals great as well as difficult to manage in a team? Let's explore each of these in turn.

Perfectionism

While it may help raise team performance, the desire to identify scope for improvement can also contribute to a joyless, soul-destroying environment. This is particularly true when per-fectionism is triggered by worries about getting it wrong, instead of the desire to make sure every next thing is better than the one before it. The difference is subtle but important. Recent research in psychology suggests that the latter is generally associated with positive experience, whereas the mistake-avoidance variety is associated with anxiety and, paradoxically but importantly, suboptimal performance. Unsurprisingly perhaps, the two are highly correlated, meaning that most of those people who aim for perfection also tend to worry a great deal about making mistakes, even if the latter tends to hamper performance and renders the overall experience much less enjoyable.[9] It creates fatigue and resistance. For that reason, sports psychologists will often spend considerable time helping athletes reframe their ambitions in terms of realizing success as opposed to avoiding failure.

Perfectionism risks creating not just an excessively critical environment but one that, perversely, places a premium on cynicism. Cynicism is often perceived as indicative of smarts and cunning, even if it is rarely helpful. Harvard Business School professor Teresa Amabile makes that point forcefully, having studied cynicism's perceived relation to intelligence. In a clever experiment, she asked people to evaluate a set of carefully crafted book reviews. When her subjects were asked to gauge the reviews, they consistently thought the writers of nasty, acerbic book reviews were more intelligent and also more competent than those who conveyed essentially the same message but in kinder ways.[10] It is one of the curiosities of team life in some societies that we find the contemptuous also the more capable, even if useless for all practical purposes.

Paranoia

The smartest of team members can be surprisingly intuitive when making choices, presumably as a result of having been right so often in the past. As with perfectionism, this is a generalization and, as with any generalization, there are plenty of exceptions.

In the workplace, high performers are often keenly aware of their worth to the team but also to the market for talent and might expect instant access to resources and the executive suite.[11] To combine intelligence with the sort of deep-seated insecurities that fuel high performance, particularly within a highly competitive milieu, can breed paranoia.

In his *Playboy* essay on the American chess player Bobby Fischer, for example, Brad Darrach describes his prodigy's media profile as "a sort of paranoid monomaniac who was terrified of girls and Russian spies but worshipped money and Spiro Agnew ... a high school dropout with a genetic kink who combined the general culture of a hard-rock deejay with a genius for spatial thinking that had made him quite possibly the greatest chess player of all time," even if he drove his support team insane.[12] Darrach's own sketch of Fischer is refreshingly forthright: "He considered himself a superstar, the strongest chess player in the world, and when it came to money, he wanted what superstars like Joe Frazer and Muhammad Ali are offered."[13]

Intel's Andy Grove's autobiography likewise leaves little to the imagination. Success, he thought, breeds complacency, and complacency failure. As the title of his book suggests, only the paranoid survive.

Tenacity

However inspiring the tenacity of baseball's Pete Reiser, his behavior risked jeopardizing the team. Having been told by his physician that he would have to sit out the remainder of the season (having once again hit the wall in attempting a catch), Reiser ripped off his bandages, snuck out of the hospital, took a train to Pittsburgh, and went to the ballpark. Upon arrival, he was told to suit up, not to play but because "it'll give 'em that little spark they need." In the fourteenth inning, however, the team had run out of pinch hitters. Reiser walked up to the bat rack, pulled out his bat, walked up to the plate, and hit a line drive over the second baseman's head—a hit that was good for three bases. With two runs scored, Reiser rounded first base and collapsed. He woke up in the hospital. He continued to play throughout the season, even if dizzy most of the time and unable to see fly balls, which might well have cost them the pennant that year.[14] Less dramatically perhaps, college basketball players, oarsmen, or gymnasts can put the health of their team members at risk by hiding illnesses for fear of deselection—something coaches are well aware of and eager to avoid.

High performers' ambition and intensity occasionally mean they can be explosive in how they deal with those around them. Having won an impressive four Premier League titles in five years with Manchester United, soccer player Eric Cantona's outbursts were as legendary as his contributions, and targeted not just at fellow teammates but at fans, too. Very few managers were willing to deal with his headstrong character.[15] Thus, in a match against London-based soccer club Crystal Palace in early 1995, Cantona was given a red card (a penalty card ejecting him) and sent off after a punishing kick on Palace defender Richard Shaw in response to Shaw pulling his shirt. As he walked toward the tunnel, he launched a kung-fu–style kick at one of Crystal Palace's taunting fans, followed by several punches. He was duly tried and found guilty of bringing "the beautiful game" in disrepute, fined, and banned for eight months. Cantona had snapped, unable to explain his own behavior: "When the hooligan called me 'a French son of a bitch' . . . I had heard it 50 billion times before. However, on that day I did not react as I used to. Why? I never found any answer to that."[16]

Self-Confidence

Despite often deep-seated insecurities, high performers are prone to overestimate the extent to which they are unique and contribute to team performance. These well-documented human traits are exacerbated in many of them. So, for example, most high school students see themselves as above average in intelligence; most business managers see themselves as more competent than average; 90 percent of motorists think themselves safer than average drivers, whereas 94 percent of university professors think themselves better than average teachers. And paradoxically, the bias of seeing ourselves as better than average causes us to see ourselves as less biased than average, too. As psychologist Daniel Gilbert points out, the tendency is not merely for us to see ourselves as more competent but as different from others, too.[17] For example, while people may see themselves as more generous than average, they also tend to see themselves as more selfish than average.

In *What Sport Tells Us About Life,* English cricketer Ed Smith credits this unusually high level of self-assurance for one of sport's more curious incidents: Zinédine Zidane's head-butting of Italy's Marco Materazzi in the 2006 World Cup final. It was, in many ways, Europe's equivalent of Mike Tyson sinking his teeth deep into Evander Holyfield's right ear. Materazzi fell to the ground. French soccer prodigy Zidane was given the red card and dismissed from the field in what should have been the swan song of a brilliant career. Everything about the event was bizarre. Zidane had already announced he would retire after the tournament, and whatever happened, he would be remembered as one of soccer's greatest players. As Smith writes: "It was almost as if a great Shakespearean actor, playing King Lear at the National Theatre for the last time, interrupted his final soliloquy by punching the dead Cordelia and then announcing his life-long hatred for producers, directors and—especially—the paying public. We all like a gracious exit. However, Zidane left us scratching our heads."[18] Unlike Tyson, Zidane never once apologized for his act of madness. Nor did he say much about what triggered his reaction except that it was an "insult to his family" made by Materazzi in the heat of the game.

In a twist to this popular explanation for his fury, Smith claims instead that Zidane acted in sheer frustration because the game had not played out as destined. Any brilliant athlete, thinks Smith, is convinced of greatness; the greater the athlete, the stronger the conviction. It can turn locker rooms into vipers' nests of egos, cliques, and fragile psyches.[19] Zidane understood that it was he who was to turn around France's fortunes in the final few minutes of the tournament, as indeed he had done before on several occasions. And so, in the 104th minute of the match, Zidane met a perfectly placed cross on his forehead, his header aiming for the top of the goal. Things were going as scripted: Zidane had already played and won a World Cup final and European Championship, having scored twice in each one, and this final, his third, was to be a replica of those two. His second goal would be France's salvation. What better moment to retire from the game he loved? Alas, Italy's goalkeeper made a superb save. Zidane's facial expression was one of unbelief: he had been denied what was rightfully his. As Smith reckons, the greater an athlete's self-belief, the greater the fall when this is punctured. So, insulted and disillusioned, Zidane blew it all.

That too much self-confidence risks reducing a team to less than the sum of its individual parts is also evident in American football. As former San Francisco 49ers Head Coach Bill Walsh explains:

> There is another side [to ego] that can wreck a team or an organization. That is being distracted by your own importance. It can come from your insecurity in working with

others. It can be the need to draw attention to yourself in the public arena. It can be a feeling that others are a threat to your own territory. These are all negative manifestations of ego, and if you are not alert to them, you get diverted and your work becomes diffused. Ego in these cases makes people insensitive to how they work with others and ends up interfering with the real goal of any group efforts.[20]

What can amount to self-delusion is hardly confined to sports. British men, for example are, on the whole, overly optimistic as to their waist sizes. A recent study points out that the average man thinks he measures 35.8 inches around the waist even if the average waist size is closer to 38 inches. This would be amusing were it not for the fact that any waist larger than 37 inches in circumference correlates with heart disease, diabetes, and cancer.[21]

Cheerier (though no less alarming) is a study reported in a March 1997 issue of *U.S. News & World Report*. One thousand Americans were given a list of names of well-known individuals, including Bill and Hilary Clinton, O. J. Simpson, Princess Diana, Oprah Winfrey, Mother Teresa, Michael Jordan, Al Gore, Pat Robertson, Newt Gingrich, Dennis Rodman, and Colin Powell. They were subsequently asked, for each of these, whether those on the list could be certain of a place in heaven. Unsurprisingly perhaps, Mother Teresa topped the list at 79 percent, followed closely by Oprah Winfrey in second place. Mr. Simpson came last at 19 percent.[22] The follow-up question was no less intriguing. What did these one thousand respondents think would happen to them after death? No less than 87 percent of them were absolutely confident of a place in heaven, effectively beating Mother Teresa to the front of the line.

Closer to our field are responses to two questions asked of 1,800 senior managers.[23] Here's the first: "On a scale of 1 to 5

(5 being "very confident," 1 being "not at all confident"), how confident are you in your own ability to make good choices?" Reassuringly, 83 percent of respondents said they were either "confident" or "very confident" of their ability to make good choices when it came to their professional lives. The second question, as usual, proved the more insightful: "How confident are you in the ability of those you work with most closely to also make good choices?" Most people anticipate that the 83 percent of self-reported self-confidence will take a beating. Few are, however, prepared for the extent of the nosedive: of the 1,800 managers surveyed, only 27 percent were either "confident" or "very confident" of the ability of their colleagues to also make good choices.

Now, of course, there is something quite ironic about this: if you happen to have been involved in hiring these colleagues, there is clearly something amiss with your ability to make good choices. That said, these survey results illustrate not just our tendency to overestimate our own abilities but, worryingly, our underestimating the abilities of others. What few seem to realize is that those we work with are often far more perceptive of being underestimated than we think they are. And, as a general rule, people resent being underestimated, particularly by those they work with every day.

It is this inferior, and often poorly grounded, assessment of the skills of others compared to one's own that can be the scourge of professional service firms. Steve Hollis, a senior partner with KPMG, has worked with a multiplicity of teams in Europe and globally. His assessment is refreshingly candid: "All too often our clients question why, with our unparalleled knowledge of their business, we can't do more to help them. All too often I find the root cause is the natural instinct to protect what we have and not risk introducing a colleague who may put all of our achievements at risk."[24]

Our relative lack of ability in many areas of life also makes us less likely to recognize when we are incompetent.[25] A nice, even if rather unusual, example of this is the story of McArthur Wheeler who, in 1995, robbed two Pittsburgh banks in broad daylight. He had made no visible attempt at disguise. Aided by surveillance tapes, the police were able to arrest him later that night. When, as part of the procedure, they showed Wheeler the video footage of him carrying out the crime, he acted in disbelief, claiming he "wore the juice." Apparently, Wheeler had been under the impression that rubbing lemon juice on one's face made one undetectable to security cameras. As the *Pittsburgh Post-Gazette* put it at the time, Wheeler might have had larceny in his heart but little in his head.[26]

But Perform They Do

Of course, not all this is bad news. If individuals didn't share at least some of these characteristics, it is unlikely that any of them (with the exception of Mr. Wheeler) would have achieved quite as much as they did. As professional service firms know particularly well, sometimes those most difficult to get along with can also be the greatest rainmakers.

A telling counterpart to soccer's Cantona and Zidane is Morgan Stanley capital markets division's Rob Parson, the protagonist of a popular Harvard Business School case study. Performance appraisals for Parson suggested his colleagues found him to be sharp-tongued, impatient, and generally just difficult to work with. Although he was an unlikely candidate, Morgan Stanley had snapped him up after a successful stint with three major investment houses. As Parson himself had already suspected, the fit was far from perfect.

While generating vast revenues for the firm, he had never quite fit the consensus-building, team-based culture of Morgan Stanley. As Paul Nasr, who recruited him, despairingly summarized: "He has created a hostile environment around him. The syndicate guys are not happy with him basically questioning their prices. The traders are not happy with him questioning their knowledge of the markets. And he always thinks he has the right answer, and the majority of the times he does have the right answer, but every time he comes up with the right answer on his own, a lot of people feel undermined."[27] Despite his rough edges, Parson was valued for his ability to cross-sell and to make introductions and share information, and for the energy he brought to bear on his work.[28]

Managing the Good with the Bad

Why is it that Cantona, Zidane, and Parson are so good and yet so bad? The answer may lie in some specific traits that, while desirable, risk derailing teams. By implication, team leadership is as much about mitigating the risks of these traits as it is about exploiting their potential. So, for example, self-belief can lead people to be more decisive, yet they risk being seen as domineering. An added dose of intelligence is useful in allowing someone to quickly grasp the complexity of the issue at hand, yet risks dismissing the contributions of others. High performers are unusually restless. As a recent survey of one hundred high achievers suggests, their single most common trait was discontent.[29] Restlessness fuels productivity. But it can cause people to be impatient with those around them as well. That they have high expectations leads them to set and achieve ambitious goals, yet can make those around them feel unable to fully satisfy expectations.

People who are disciplined are useful insofar as they foster efficiency and productivity, yet they risk being accused of entertaining unrealistic expectations. Their charisma can help bring out the best in others, yet they risk being manipulative in luring others into particular ways of doing things. They are determined to win and hate getting the short end of the stick, meaning they often end up getting what they want. And yet because everything becomes a competition of sorts, their behavior can be threatening to their peers. They are often tenacious but can drive others to exhaustion. Unafraid of change, and lured by the promise of newness, they risk taking action before the requisite buy-in of colleagues. Their farsightedness is valuable in discovering whatever gaps there are between today and tomorrow but often at the expense of focusing on what needs to be done now. The strength of their convictions makes them believable but can cause them to become defensive when challenged.[30]

Talent Q Group has compiled assessment data from over fourteen thousand individuals adding further traits that risk derailing teams when under pressure: hypersensitivity, as a result of being overly anxious and often surprisingly fragile emotionally; isolation, particularly when also being poor communicators; iconoclasm, or being willing to break with convention but, in doing so, being insensitive to those around them; attention-seeking behavior, making them prone to exaggerating; and, as in Steve Jobs's case, a tendency to micromanage the affairs of others.[31]

Thus, high performers oscillate between healthy and irritating behaviors. As Work Ethic's Kate Ludeman and Eddie Erlandson write, "their magnetic leadership commands respect, but their aggressive tactics create resistance, resentment and revenge. They are celebrated for their achievements but loathed for the carnage they leave in their wake. People stand in awe of their competence and can-do energy, but they often hate reporting to them or teaming with them."[32]

Many employees nowadays spend ten or more hours a month complaining about their bosses (or listening to similar complaints by others), while around one-third spent twenty hours doing so, and occasionally far more.[33] Internet blogs are a rich source of such complaints. Take this one for example:

> [My boss] pays me $20 hr to basically take messages on lit-
> tle scraps of paper (I'm not allowed to have a message
> book) and write up invoices, etc that he dictates word for
> word and totals in Excel, so he can verify how Quickbook
> calculates! But I am called the office manager and referred
> to as "her." He insults the crew and customers all day,
> every day. He's taken a successful company and has ruined
> it by changing everything that worked to "his way" ... he's
> totally inconsistent ... messes up everything, wastes every-
> one's time ... This is the worse case of a clueless, control
> freak narcissist I have ever encountered and I'm 58 years
> old. He plays on the computer all day, crunches Fritos
> (loudly) burps, sneezes, sighs constantly ... spits tobacco in
> the garbage cans & bathroom sink. I have never heard him
> say excuse me. Rather, the bigger the burp, the prouder he
> is.[34]

Robert Sutton's *The No Asshole Rule* pulls no punches either. His arsenal includes studies of U.S. nurses as recipients of verbal abuse from physicians. One of these, conducted in 1997 and written up in the *Journal of Professional Nursing,* found that 90 percent of the 130 nurses surveyed reported being victims of verbal abuse over the previous twelve months. A similar study published in *Orthopaedic Nursing* surveyed 461 nurses of whom 91 percent reported similar complaints, but within a single month.[35]

The Leadership Challenge

So it seems we cannot have our cake and eat it too. Or can we? A first step is surely to acknowledge the risks entailed in our own behavior, and to set clear limits as to what behavior is and isn't acceptable on the team. The risk of an individual derailing a team can be mitigated by helping him to realize that his behavior may ultimately thwart his own potential.

Duke University's legendary coach Mike Krzyzewski holds "irritant meetings," challenging his staff and players to think of as many irritants as possible and—in the spirit of "let's not let Duke beat Duke"—to have them out in the open for discussion. The complaints can be something as simple as bad food or accommodation, tardiness of one or more team members, inflammatory language, personal hygiene, sloppiness, lack of engagement or perceived lack of commitment, or even someone not speaking out when they should.[36]

Like the proverbial dead fish under the boardroom table, if you leave it there long enough, it will start to stink. Anecdotal observations suggest that conversations and meetings like Krzyzewski's can be helped by relying on "hard facts" insofar as objective data feeds the analytical part of the brain.[37] By their very nature, high performers are uncomfortable exposing their insecurities. To substantiate this, we need look no further than the proliferation of "corporate coaches" who are engaged, often confidentially, to help senior executives come to terms with their inner demons. Sports teams have long done likewise by retaining the services of sports psychologists.

Team Bonding

Aware of the risk of derailment, those tasked with leading teams have often resorted to "away days," retreats, or corporate team-bonding exercises. Chances are that you have already thrown considerable resources at team-building exercises: trivia nights, military-style boot camps, treasure hunts, wine tastings, traversing hot coals, building towers from bits of trash, or tracking down fugitives, their variety limited only to the human imagination and corporate budget. Their effects are often short-lived, and their consequences occasionally costly.

Athletes too seek out team-building events, even though the events can polarize as much as bond. Former Australian cricketer, Shane Warne, recommends against them, worried about the injuries they might cause. "I am from the old school," he says. "If you want to gel everyone together, lock them up in a pub and do not let anyone come in. Sometimes after a long summer of cricket, players are better off spending time away from each other so they can recharge the batteries. Not a boot camp."[38] Steve Waugh, his former captain, disagrees: "To me, 'bonding' is an overrated term normally linked to reminiscing about past escapades with a truck-load of grog on board. I've had my fair share of these nights, and while they can create a few laughs and a better understanding of each other, the experience is shallow and soon forgotten."[39]

To make sure they are not shallow, the events occasionally include periods of collective reflection, such as the Australian cricket team's trip to Gallipoli and the Somme, or the England cricket team's visit to Flanders Field and Dachau.[40] England captain Andrew Strauss's description of the bonding experience as a "tough but rewarding five days" took on more meaning when the England and Wales Cricket Board publicly confirmed that one of the team, James Anderson, had suffered a cracked rib during a boxing match against another teammate.[41] Then again, the England team did go on to win the 2010 Ashes, arguably cricket's most famous prize.

Occasionally, the exercises get bizarre. Take, for example, Alarm One Inc.'s decision to pit sales teams against each other in an exercise where the winners would poke fun at the losers, throwing pies at them, feeding them baby food, making them wear diapers, and swatting their buttocks. One "losing" employee, Janet Orlando, subsequently sued the California home security company for having spanked her with a competitor's yard sign; the company ended up paying $1.7 million for the privilege. Or consider the example of Chad Hudgens, until recently employed by Utah-based motivational coaching firm Prosper Inc. After volunteering for a new but undisclosed team-building exercise, he was taken outside and pinned to the ground by colleagues before his enterprising boss proceeded to pour water all over his face, telling Hudgens's team members all the while that he wanted them to work as hard on sales as Hudgens did at breathing. Needless to say, Hudgens has since sued his employer.

As a correspondent for the *Times of London* writes: "Nobody worries about team spirit on the factory floor. You never see teams of assembly-line workers scaling rock faces in East London . . . Only the pretentious and the terminally short of ideas feel that there is anything to be gained from being strapped into a canoe with some halfwit from marketing, and having an ex-commando bark instructions at you for a day."[42]

More auspicious perhaps is a recent study by three University of California–Berkeley psychologists on the effect of touch on team performance. By coding the touch behavior of 294 players from all thirty National Basketball Association (NBA) teams during the 2008–2009 season, they discovered that frequent touching early on predicted greater performance for teams as well as individuals later in the season. When controlling for player status, preseason expectations, and early season performance, their hypothesis that touch predicted improved performance still held. Intuitively this makes sense. By touching—using high fives, chest bumps, leaping shoulder bumps, chest punches, head slaps, head grabs, low fives, high tens, full hugs, half hugs, and team huddles—we communicate cooperation, and help lay to rest the anxieties experienced by others in communicating affect, reassurance, and trust.[43] The practicalities of generalizing these findings to the bank, law firm, or boardroom, however, are less clear-cut.

The "Stephens Question"

A more promising antidote is that of galvanizing teams around a credible cause. And here is where sporting teams often have it over their corporate cousins. The Cambridge University Boat Club (CUBC) has always had a single objective. Founded in 1828 by two students, one from the University of Oxford, the other from Cambridge University, the club's goal remains that of beating Oxford in the annual Boat Race. This race is still rowed "at or near London, each in an eight-oared boat during the Easter vacation" in full view of the public. As the second-oldest varsity match in the world (cricket predates it by one year), it attracts a quarter of a million people on the banks of the River Thames and a television audience of an estimated 120 million around the world.

The question as to why this student race should hold such universal appeal is itself interesting: Is it because it involves two of the world's grandest institutions of learning, the intellectual homes of Lewis Carroll, John Maynard Keynes, W. H. Auden, Stephen Hawking, and C. S. Lewis? Is it the secrecy surrounding crew selection and race preparation? Is it because rowing has mostly remained an amateur sport, meaning that either university crew will often field Olympians and world champions? Or is it because it has always been a thing of sharp contrasts: passionately amateur and yet holding to professional standards, a world of mutual respect yet intense rivalry, where it's all about taking part but where the pain of losing is intolerable?

Perhaps it is the all-or-nothing character of the race, as four-time Olympic gold medalist Matthew Pinsent explains: "You must have huge courage to put yourself through all that is required to earn your seat, and row the race. There's something very alluring about putting yourself through all that, in order to row a race where the prize is a small medal in a little box. The pain is so worthwhile, but the penalties for losing are really high too. In other walks of life there is much to achieve even if you don't win, whereas in the Boat Race it's all or nothing."[44]

Few workplaces can compete with as compelling and simple a purpose. It allows the CUBC to strip complex, often highly emotive decisions to their bare bones. They call it the "Stephens Question," so-named after an influential former club manager, Roger Stephens: "Will doing this make the boat faster?" The answer is ultimately a straightforward yes or no. Notwithstanding the fact that most workplaces are vastly more complex in their pursuit of multiple objectives, would it help to try and distill, at the level of the team, an equivalent of a Stephens Question? The predictable, "Will this increase shareholder value?" may be the correct test as far as senior management or corporate boards are concerned but it is unlikely to inspire. The real question is what will.

In sum, stars appear to be important to teams. Does this mean you can take a team populated with nothing but stars and expect over-the-top results? Apparently not, as the next chapter will show.

2

Why Inequality Is a Good Thing

The Old: On true teams, everyone is equal.

The New: On high-performance teams, everyone is not equal.

The Challenge: How to manage inequality in teams.

Are teams really more than the sum of their parts? The sobering evidence suggests that teams rarely produce synergies, with a string of academic studies finding that individuals clearly outperform teams. How then can teams create value? Theoretically, of course, much like any form of human organization: by reducing the costs of coordinating between individuals and by combining resources or skill sets. Teams do not usually create value by getting the best resources their money can buy but, rather, by *combining* resources into something of which the value exceeds the economic cost.

Thus, during the 1996 Football (soccer) World Cup, the Italian team was more than the sum of its parts, whereas the Brazilian team was not.[1] And arguably the same can be said for the 2010 Football World Cup teams of England, France, and Italy. England fielded some of the world's best soccer talent—Wayne Rooney, Steven Gerrard, Rio Ferdinand, Ashley Cole, and Frank Lampard among them—yet they failed to live up to their reputations and salaries. They managed, as one newspaper put it, to orchestrate a comically unwatchable game against a side dismissed as the worst in the 2010 World Cup in their very first match. The journalist, Marina Hyde, took no prisoners:

> One can only observe, yet again, how perfectly good, even excellent players seem automatically to malfunction the minute they don the accursed garment. The England shirt is the precise opposite of a superhero costume, turning men with extraordinary abilities into mild-mannered guys next door. Were Stephen Fry to pull it on, he would struggle to string a sentence together. Were Lucian Freud to slip it over his head he would turn his easel round to reveal a childlike scribble of a cat. Psychological meltdown is now part of the warp and weft of its wretched fibers and it will clearly take someone other than Capello [the England head coach] to fix it.[2]

Sporting history is piteously rich in such examples of under-performing star-studded teams. In 2004, a team featuring LeBron James and former MVP Allen Iverson became the first U.S. men's basketball team to lose in Olympic play since NBA players joined the Games in 1992. The team, of course, was juvenile (the average age being 23.6 years old), and several superstars had passed on the chance to play (nine of twelve players from the 2003 team had elected not to play in Athens, including Karl Malone, Tracy

McGrady, and Jason Kidd). Still, their pedigree had led many to expect them to take home far more than a bronze medal.[3]

Their substandard display was particularly disappointing given a humiliating sixth-place finish at the 2002 FIBA World Championships, and led USA Basketball to kick-start a long-term project aimed at restoring their pride by creating better and more cohesive teams. The 2004 defeat marked only the third time that a U.S. men's basketball team failed to win gold (when the 1980 Moscow Olympics boycott is not included), and the first losing team to have fielded professionals. Things fared little better during the 2006 FIBA World Championships, when a team of twelve NBA stars propped up by several successful coaches lost to Greece.

Likewise, in the inaugural World Baseball Classic of 2006, which pitted national teams from sixteen countries to play each other in a series of round robins, the United States fielded some talented players—Roger Clemens, Derek Jeter, Alex Rodriguez, and Johnny Damon to name a few—in what is the ultimate American game. Yet it failed to make the semifinals, ending up in eighth place after Venezuela, Mexico, South Korea, and Japan (which won the tournament).[4]

Across the pond, one of the brawniest-ever British men's relay teams missed out on gold in the 1996 Olympic Games. While silver may be an admirable feat in and of itself, one of the runners, Mark Richardson, still firmly believes that a gold medal was well within reach. After all, his six-strong relay squad was in stunning shape, having never had athletes run so consistently and so well: all were able to dispatch 400 meters in under forty-five seconds. And they had every right to be confident of beating the United States after American Michael Johnson got hurt in his record-breaking 200-meter sprint. Brewing within the squad, however, had been a public spat between two of Britain's fastest runners, Roger Black and Du'aine Ladejo. In a press conference before the British

Olympic trials, Ladejo avowed that he would break Black's 400-meter British record, an initiative to which Black responded by betting Ladejo £1,000 (about $1,500) that he wouldn't.

As it happened, Black won the bet, but the rivalry—usually the preserve of 100-meter sprinters—carried over to the Olympic squad. Moreover, the coaches postponed their decision on exactly which four runners would compete in the relay race until the eve of the final. "We never did have much of a chance to become a team," Richardson noted. We knew what had to be done, and what success would look like, but we never engaged at a personal level. There never was an opportunity to talk about the stuff we worried might unsettle us, the things we were afraid might happen and how we would deal with them as a team; of how we could help each other overcome our insecurities. We never did get to this deeper level, and I suspect that's what kept us from taking home gold."[5]

That said, there are some good examples of the whole exceeding the sum of its parts, too. None of Liverpool's successes in English soccer during the 1970s and 1980s are attributable to the brilliance of a single player. As sports journalist Jim White surmised: "There is no question that the one-for-all, all-for-one mentality generated in the Anfield dressing room was the engine that drove the great team. With players such as Alan Kennedy, John Wark, Sammy Lee and Craig Johnston, nobody could claim this was a collection of top-notch operators in the manner, say, of the current Real Madrid. Every week, they played as an entity greater than the sum of its parts."[6]

Manchester United's Sir Alex Ferguson voices similar sentiments: "In my business, togetherness is not just a nice concept that you can take or leave according to taste. If you don't have it, you are nothing. Selfishness, factionalism, clique-ishness are all death to a football team. As a manager in football, I have never been interested in simply sending out a collection of brilliant individuals. There is no substitute for talent but, on the field, talent without unity of purpose is a hopelessly devalued currency."[7] True to his principles, Sir Alex had no compunction whatsoever in releasing the club's star player, David Beckham, after a "dressing room incident."

The England soccer squad of 1966—the last to win the World Cup—sacrificed some of its star players, like Jimmy Greaves, in favor of others who were thought to benefit the squad's cohesion. Likewise, the French 4 ×100 meter relay team famously set a world record with a time of 37.79 seconds in the 1990 European championships despite having not a single individual title among them. Based on their individual times, none would have made a 100-meter Olympic final.[8] And, of course, one could easily argue that the United States has been able to field "dream teams" since 1992 and has taken home more gold medals than any other nation (thirteen in sixteen Olympic tournaments), and that, more often than not, these star-studded teams have got it right.

So where does this leave us on the question of "stars" or "no stars" as it relates to team performance? If, as the previous chapter suggested, some stars are useful for teams, how many is too many? Is inequality in talent, reputation, and remuneration (as is typically the case when stars adorn teams) a good or bad thing?

Inequality in Remuneration

Basketball and soccer serve as useful examples in that they feature some of sport's highest payrolls. According to Cornell University labor economist Lawrence Kahn, the four major U.S. team sports employ around three thousand to four thousand athletes who, in the mid-1990s, earned some $600,000 on average in ice hockey,

$650,000 in American football, $1.2 million in baseball, and $1.8 million in basketball, or well in excess of the 1997 average earnings of full-time, full-year equivalent workers of around $25,000.[9] These pay differentials prompt some tricky questions: What really is the relation between money and team performance? Is performance more likely to be a function of absolute pay, or what players are paid relative to team members?

The evidence to date suggests that, at least in the English soccer league, teams with the highest payroll also do well in terms of performance. So too in European soccer more widely: Barcelona and Real Madrid have now overtaken the New York Yankees as the best-paid global sports teams, paying its players £7.9 million and £7.4 million, respectively, compared to £6.8 million for the Yankees baseball players on average. When he compared payrolls and league rankings for forty English soccer clubs over two decades, sports economist Stefan Szymanski noted that payrolls account for as much as 92 percent of the variation in league positions. Repeating the exercise for Italy, the correlation was a solid 93 percent.[10] In baseball, too, comparisons of payrolls suggest that payroll and performance are highly correlated. There are, of course, some legendary exceptions: Billy Beane's Oakland A's punched well above their weight for several baseball seasons, performing to a level usually associated with clubs with three times the payroll.[11]

Might it be that the size of the overall payroll alone is less important to team performance than discrepancies between salaries in a single team? A polemic study by three University of North Dakota academics suggests that baseball teams with substantial differences among players' salaries tend to perform better than those in which players are paid more or less equally. In the sample of thirty baseball teams from the National and American Leagues between 2002 and 2006, teams with many average-paid players performed much less well than those with significant disparities between those at the bottom and top ends of the pay scale. The study implies that however attractive equalized pay might be from an ideological point of view, it makes no sense from a team perspective. A handful of generously paid star players may help raise the performance of even those less well compensated.[12]

Beyond baseball, however, the evidence gets murky. A similar study of professional ice hockey finds a negative relation between pay inequality and performance.[13] In a more recent analysis of professional basketball, economists David Berri and Todd Jewell find no correlation whatsoever between differences in pay among team members and team performance.[14]

Comparative studies of the workplace are no more insightful. Proponents of salary compression argue that equal pay enhances cooperation, which leads to synergies, which, in turn, increase collective performance.[15] Other studies, typically by labor economists, suggest that, as in baseball, wage disparity can indeed improve team performance.[16] Here the suggestion is that pay inequality results in higher worker productivity, with those on the bottom rung willing to accept comparatively low wages in the hope of ultimately securing one of the few coveted, more generously remunerated positions at the top of the organizational hierarchy. Inequality, in other words, provides an incentive to work hard for the team, as team performance and individual career progression are intimately and inextricably tied together. Adam Smith would be pleased.

Inequality in Talent

Individual stars can have a disproportionate effect on team performance, as we saw in chapter 1. Is it possible to have too many stars on the team?

In an insightful piece of research, Boris Groysberg and colleagues suggest there are strong diminishing returns to hiring stars, at least in investment banking. Their dataset comprised annual rankings of sell-side equity research analysts, published between 1996 and 2001 in *Institutional Investor*; it is useful insofar as it contains a relatively objective ranking of some six thousand analysts through polls and surveys of investment officers, money managers, and institutional investors. These analysts are highly paid for what they do, many of them taking home more than $1 million a year. To this list, Groysberg added information supplied by a Greenwich Associates institutional research services survey on three thousand client respondents. The analysis strongly suggests that star performers (or those included in *Institutional Investor*'s All-America Research Team) did increase their team's overall effectiveness. Here, Groysberg's findings corroborate what we learned in chapter 1.

But, say Groysberg and his colleagues, they increase overall performance only up to a point. Beyond this, any additional star recruited reversed this direction and hurt team performance. This tipping point varied by type of organization. So, for example, firms seen by clients as exhibiting particularly high levels of expertise, such as Morgan Stanley, found that collective performance begins to suffer when the proportion of stars versus average players exceeds 44.6 percent. (The beauty of the sample is, of course, the ease of measuring performance.) This was different for those groups blessed with average analysts where performance didn't drop until 70 percent of a group reached star level. Beyond these levels, stars stop sharing information, while demanding ever-higher salaries.[17]

Isn't it then curious that sports and business alike continue to pay excessively for star talent, even, if necessary, by purchasing entire, albeit relatively small organizations? For example, Facebook,

Google, and Zynga have all satisfied their hunger for talent by buying start-ups to get their founders and engineers, while discarding their products. Even though software development is hardly ever a solitary effort, Facebook acquired FriendFeed for $47 million, principally to access its stock of twenty software engineers, as well as Drop.io (to get its hands on Sam Lessin), Hot Potato (for Justin Shaffer), and Nextstop (for Carl Sjogreen).[18]

Moreover, there are plenty of teams that have done well by growing their own talent. Take FC Barcelona. In 2009, it became the first-ever club to win six out of six competitions in a single season: La Liga, Copa del Rey, Champions League, Spanish Super Cup, UEFA Super Cup, and FIFA Club World Cup. As one of the world's finest soccer teams, "Barça" has its fair share of star players, Lionel Messi, Andres Iniesta, and David Villa among them. What is interesting is that eight of its leading players are entirely homegrown. The club features its own La Masia academy with a curriculum that greatly emphasizes character development. Here students are taught that "Barça is 'more than a club': it is the embodiment of Catalan pride that kept the region's spirit alive during the years when Spain groaned under the fascist Franco regime."[19]

But, of course, research analysts working under the same roof are not teams in quite the same way the San Francisco 49ers or Philadelphia 76ers are. American football and basketball require far greater degrees of interdependence and complementary skills. And yet here, too, star performance can be detrimental. When, in 1995, Michael Jordan decided to return to basketball after a brief courtship in baseball with the Chicago White Sox, the unintended consequence of the superstar rejoining the Chicago Bulls players was to disrupt whatever team dynamics had developed in his absence. Croatian small forward Toni Kukoč had been terribly disappointed when Jordan announced his retirement shortly after

Kukoč was drafted by the Bulls, and now he was too intimidated to go one-on-one against Jordan in practice. Likewise, Steve Kerr, one of NBA's most accurate three-point shooters, quickly deferred to Jordan's experience. As then–head coach Phil Jackson writes in *Sacred Hoops*:

> Once Michael officially joined the team and started playing in games, the situation didn't improve. Some of the players were so bedazzled by his moves they'd unconsciously step back and wait to see what he was going to do next. And Michael was so absorbed in his struggle to prove to himself that he still had the touch, he often made uncharacteristic misjudgments. To make matters worse, his teammates were reluctant to make demands on him. In one game, Michael missed Steve Kerr, who was wide open in the corner, and drove to the hoop, only to get clobbered by three defenders. Kerr was the best three-point shooter in the league last year. When Michael went to the free throw line, I asked Steve to inform Michael that he was open, and Steve looked at me and shrugged his shoulders. There was no way he was going to tell the great Michael Jordan how to play the game.[20]

Capitalizing on Differences in Individual Talent, Pay, and Personality

So, how do you get the best from star performers? Or, if not the best, then how can you mitigate any negative impact they have on the teams they join? Here, too, Groysberg and colleagues provide some useful suggestions. Rather than treating the Bobby Fischers of this world as solo performers, you should surround them with high-quality colleagues. The point is to create a so-called "Matthew effect," a term from sociology meaning, essentially, the rich get richer, while the poor get poorer: stars will attract other stars or help create future stars.

At Goldman Sachs, for example, management concentrates the development of a high-quality sales force in-house to complement the organization's star analysts. According to Groysberg et al., "As a result, Goldman Sachs salespeople are not just vital in getting clients to accept and act on analysts' reports; they also help the analysts to perform at a higher level. A salesperson might, for instance, ask the analysts thoughtful, perceptive questions that will help them sharpen and refine their thinking. Or the salesperson might relay important client feedback that could provide the analysts with important insights."[21] Moreover, companies could do worse than prioritize the development of talent in-house. After all, in-house opportunities provide some distinct advantages: the realization that management is interested in their development might lead people to increase their efforts and commitment to the organization. This loyalty can pay off as competitors court star performers and, particularly when widely known, may ensure that the organization becomes the employer of choice for raw talent.

Michael Jordan appears to have been keenly aware of his need for a strong support team. After scoring fifty-five points in a game against the New York Knicks, he asked Jackson to tell the team to up their game instead of waiting for him to save the night. And it is to Jackson's and Jordan's great credit—Jackson for his Zenlike approach to coaching and Jordan for his coachability—that they were able to create an unbeatable team out of such strong personalities as Scottie Pippin, Horace Grant, and "Dennis the Menace" Rodman. Jackson is crystal-clear in his approach to manufacturing consent among strong personalities: get them to connect with something larger than themselves.[22] This caters to a core need that the most coveted credit cards or largest salaries are unable to fill. Says Jackson, "Even for those who don't consider themselves 'spiritual' in a conventional sense, creating a successful team—whether it's an NBA champion or a record-setting sales force—is essentially a spiritual act."[23]

The McLaren Group's CEO Ron Dennis expects that same level of connection in his organization: "If you've worked here for three months and you don't bleed McLaren then you're in the wrong company. If you want to work here, you have to be prepared to identify totally with our values and understand that good isn't good enough. We take ownership of every piece of equipment, your desk and your environment because when we come to work we want to excel. I love what I do, I'm passionate about it and I want to see that same passion in my employees."

But how then do you sustain passion, particularly in austere times and in nonsporting environments? Can you prevent indifference from spreading like an open sore? To this, Dennis has a reply: "The easiest thing is simply to sign another check. Not only is this not always possible, it is often better to give people your time; it is the most valuable commodity I have."[24] Saatchi & Saatchi's deputy chairman Richard Hytner shares Dennis's viewpoint. At his firm, senior executives like himself make a point of spending face time with those lower down the career ladder, particularly during periods of economic austerity when resources are hard to come by.

To foster a sense of passion in his 2010 European Ryder Cup team, golfer Colin Montgomery relied on his close friend Seve Ballesteros, who was one of the great swashbuckling golf heroes of the eighties and nineties. In an interview shortly after Ballesteros's death, Montgomery talked about Ballesteros's passion for the game, which had inspired so many professional golfers around the world to take up the sport and bring it to new levels. Ballesteros was largely responsible for making the Ryder Cup a global phenomena. It was also Ballesteros who is due much of the credit for significant increases in the levels of prize money, given the sport's popularity. When Ballesteros was not well enough to be at Celtic Manor for the 2010 Ryder Cup, Montgomery arranged a team conference call with him. The team was made up of twelve of the finest golfers in Europe—six of whom were rookies to the Ryder Cup—and Montgomery wanted them to experience Ballesteros's passion for the contest that they were about to play. After their victory, Montgomery fittingly credited their half-point winning margin to Ballesteros's inspiration.

Canadian international rugby player Matt Guinness-King has his own version of this inspiration: a quote by Antoine de Saint-Exupéry: "If you want to build a ship, don't teach the workers to find the wood and saw it and nail the boards together; teach them how to love the seas."[25]

Lovable Fools and Competent Jerks

Of course, not all teams are privileged to have a Phil Jackson, Sir Alex Ferguson, or Colin Montgomery at the helm. Or even a Michael Sherwood (Goldman Sachs) or Gary Kelly (Southwest Airlines), corecipients of *HR* magazine's 2010 Excellence Award for Most People-Focused CEO. In fact, the ability to gel a group of individual high performers into something greater than the sum of its parts may need to come from within. If so, this raises an interesting conundrum: are there competencies beyond individual technical qualities that can significantly enhance the performance of a team? For instance, can social or emotional intelligence (despite difficulties of measurement) help raise performance levels in even technically the most demanding environments?

Tackling these questions head on in provocative academic research, Tiziana Casciaro and Miguel Sousa Lobo arrived at some interesting findings.[26] Their study honed in on four very different types of organizations: a Silicon Valley start-up, a business unit of a multinational IT corporation, a North American university, and the Spanish country office of a global luxury-goods corporation. They also incorporated responses from their MBA students, collecting data on more than ten thousand workplace relationships. Respondents characterized each of these in terms of how much they liked (or disliked) working with specific colleagues, and how well they thought these individuals did their jobs.

So how did those who are technically passable and also likable stack up against colleagues who are far more competent but unpleasant to be around? The analysis suggests that if someone is strongly disliked, it is almost irrelevant whether or not he is competent. By contrast, if someone is liked, her colleagues will seek out every bit of competence she has to offer, meaning that a little likability has far more mileage than competence in making someone a desirable team member. Even if someone is competent, those around him may feel reluctant to reveal their vulnerabilities if he intimidates, belittles their contributions, or never pays any attention to them. Add to this the suggestion that corporate clients are by and large unable to identify slight differences in ability (in that they are unlikely to tell the difference between an employment lawyer being 94 percent or 98 percent competent), social competence would appear to win out over its technical counterpart.

KPMG's Steve Hollis frames this trade-off as the 80–20 rule. In his experience, professionals typically rate their technical excellence as accounting for 80 percent of their success, with the remaining 20 percent due to the quality of their relationships with clients: "The dichotomy is that the very same clients take the professional's technical excellence for granted and the dominant determining factor is the quality of the relationship. This should not come as any great surprise: for most professionals their progression to greatness is built on their ability to absorb technical material. It is what they have spent most of their working lives aiming to achieve. As sport and business consistently demonstrate, technical excellence alone rarely results in 2 + 2 = 5."[27] For Brendan Purcell, head coach of GB Canoeing, social competence at its minimum entails the ability to give feedback to team members and receive it. In world-class canoeing, as in many team sports, the fastest individual athletes need not also make for the fastest crew boat.

Despite the variety of organizations represented in Casciaro and Sousa Lobo's sample, it is easy to think of environments in which competence should trump likability pretty much all the time: aviation, aerospace, surgery, law, and traffic control, for example. A client faced with a complex legal battle may need a team of lawyers to simultaneously provide such specialist competencies as taxation, real estate, intellectual property, and cross-border experience. Thus, the more complex the task, the wider the range of expertise required. Also, much would depend on the abilities of team leaders to manage difficult behaviors, and on who else is already on the team.

We could argue that the more important the task, the more weight is placed on competence. If, God forbid, you suffer from a heart condition, chances are that you'd much prefer to be seen by the country's best cardiologist than by a socially more gifted but technically less competent colleague. If so, you might be surprised to learn that physicians are more likely to persist with a difficult diagnosis (including yours) when they like their patients. Conversely, they will likely settle for a standard diagnosis when they do not. And they make up their minds about us as quickly as we do about them. As a general rule, doctors like the sickest patients least, note Northeastern University social psychologist Judy Hall and Johns Hopkins' Debra Roter, if only because diseases that resist even the best therapies can leave the doctors with a deep sense of personal failure. In a long series of studies on physicians and patient relationships, Hall and Roter link feelings of like and dislike to doctors' abilities to listen and think: those who disliked their patients were more likely to cut them off during a recitation of symptoms and settle for a convenient diagnosis to which they became more committed with the passing of time.[28]

How might this trade-off between social and technical competence play itself out in sports? Here it may be worthwhile to explore a single example in some detail. When, in early January 2007, the chief coach of the Cambridge University Boat Club announced the lineup of what he thought would make for the fastest combination of eight oarsmen to race Oxford in the quintessential Boat Race, five of the selected oarsmen rebelled. All five had rowed, and lost, the race the previous year. Two of them, Tom James and Sebastian Schulte, asked to see the chief coach in private, telling him he had made a terrible mistake in not including Canadian Dan O'Shaughnessy. Even though they knew full well that he was technically less able than the rower he would replace—and almost exactly as powerful—they were convinced O'Shaughnessy would be able to help them to collectively raise their game. By virtue of his brash yet lighthearted personality and social skills, they considered him uniquely able to defuse conflict in the crew and silence some of its stronger members. Moreover, he made calls while racing that seemed to have a marked effect on the crew's ability to coordinate. In rowing, coordination means speed.

What few of them realized at the time was that O'Shaughnessy's calls typically originated with Kip McDaniel, a fellow Canadian and prodigy of America's legendary college-rowing coach, Harry Parker. McDaniel had stroked the Blue Boat (the crew of eight that races Oxford each year in the Boat Race) in 2006 and, as the leading man, took a disproportionate amount of the blame for having lost the race. Given this, his teammates would not likely appreciate his calls. Yet he also knew the stretch of water between Putney and Mortlake better than almost anyone. So he would tell O'Shaughnessy what to say; O'Shaughnessy, in turn, made the relevant calls. Cambridge's chief coach gave in to James and Schulte; he removed a more gifted oarsman and had O'Shaughnessy, technically less competent, take his seat.

Of course, we will never know whether the crew might have also won the race with their original lineup. O'Shaughnessy stayed on for two more years but never made the Blue Boat crew again. The following year was an Olympic year, and typically the best oarsmen return home to train with the national squads. This left both Oxford and Cambridge with crews that were less experienced and socially more cohesive. O'Shaughnessy's social skills were now less relevant, and his lack of technical ability became a disadvantage in selection.

Recent rowing history entails another, more poignant example of the trade-off between social and technical competence. Bobby Thatcher had been a member of the squad that produced Britain's Olympic gold-winning eight in 2000. Having trained twenty years to become an Olympic champion, he was dropped from Britain's squad only a month before the Sydney Games were to start, even though he had outperformed others on the water. Thatcher's story, retold in Josh Raymond's beautiful essay for *Prospect,* recounts the pressure, ambiguity, and raw emotion wrapped up in crew selection. Despite his performance during trials, Thatcher failed to make the final eight, for reasons that were never clear to him. Simon Dennis, who successfully ended up rowing in the 2000 Games, hadn't beat Thatcher in a boat all year, even though he was a little quicker on the rowing machine. Thatcher resented this. He claimed Dennis got in because he, along with two others, had rowed in their coach's eight at Imperial College, London. One of these, Luka Grubor, was injured all season and, according to Thatcher, didn't even make the trial. "They never gave me a good reason," he says, "just told me the way I rowed didn't fit in."[29]

So why was Thatcher not selected? Raymond's account of Thatcher's bid for Olympic gold provides a number of clues. "The selection was based on ergometer testing, small boats performance and racing different combinations at the World Cup regattas," he quotes coach Martin McElroy as saying. "There were arguably twelve people who would have been capable of winning in that boat. Bobby was a dedicated athlete but had a history of immature behavior." Rowley Douglas, coxswain of the Olympic crew, explained:

> Bob was the nice guy at the party, always cracking jokes, but if he knew when to stop then he didn't show it. We used to carry the blades down together, and when a football had been washed up by the tide we'd kick it about a bit. Martin told me one day that I needed to be more focused on the rowing so I stopped, but Bobby was still out there every morning looking for footballs. He turned up on time and did all his stretching, so I think he thought it didn't matter . . . Everyone has to be on the same page psychologically . . . and it was a really close call. Ultimately, though, if there are two cars that both have the same engine, then you're going to pick the color you like. Bobby never tried to be the color the coaches liked.[30]

Thatcher's technical superiority was unable to compensate for what coaches felt was his possible lack of commitment or social cohesion.

For Thatcher, the sheer impact of being dropped from the squad was hugely significant at a personal level. After a short stint moving furniture in a warehouse (while his former crew was celebrating their Olympic success), Thatcher took a job in sales. As he recalls: "They gave me these business cards that said 'Rob Thatcher' on them. I told them my name was Bobby, and they said they'd decided that Rob sounded more businesslike. I looked at that card and wanted to cry. I should have been an Olympic champion, and here was this guy in a cheap button-down shirt deciding he could change my name."

Difficulties of Measurement

Perhaps the real issue in the O'Shaughnessy and Thatcher examples is not really just a simple matter of trading competence for likability. Maybe what's at stake here is the difficulty of taking rationally defensible and comprehensive measures of performance: the ability of certain individuals to provide depth of experience, to defuse conflict, to provide social cohesion or even that much-needed stimulus to competition within the team. Simply put, the impact that individuals have on those around them may be difficult to measure objectively but is nonetheless a crucially important input in the manufacture of synergy.

The difficulty here is how to measure not just individual ability but the contribution of someone to the larger team, taking into account that he or she can enhance as well as inhibit the performance of those on the team. Again, sports seem to have the edge over business. Basketball coaches, for example, use something called "plus-minus," or a measure of any given player's effect when on the court. A good player might average three points more per game than others, meaning he's a plus 3. Thus, Steve Nash was a plus 14.5, Shane Battier a plus 10, and Tracy McGrady a plus 6.[31]

Crew coaches like to use a technique called "seat racing," where two four-man crews of similar strength will race each other over a stipulated distance. The coach notes the respective finishing times of both crews. After the first race, two oarsmen, one from each crew, swap places, and the crews race each other again. This process of swapping oarsmen after every race is repeated until everyone has swapped places with his or her counterpart at least once. Given that the speed of a boat depends not just on the application of power but of power applied consistently by a seamlessly coordinated crew, the only way to win a seat race is to perfectly synchronize with the other three oarsmen in the crew. Rowers have no choice but to fluctuate between viewing a fellow oarsman first as foe, then as friend, as they strive to cooperate flawlessly with someone who was a competitor just minutes earlier.[32] But the technique achieves its aim, namely, objectively isolating the effect of a single individual on a crew.

To systematically recombine individuals in a controlled experiment is far more difficult in the workplace. That said, professional service firms regularly use something similar in recruitment and selection. Groups typically face off on a series of problem-solving challenges; candidates rotate between groups until they've reached an optimal combination or, more likely, until the impact of single individuals on the rest of the team becomes clear. An obvious problem is controlling for the exercise's level of difficulty, since the same exercise cannot be used twice, and deciding on a uniform measure of success. The exercise is also time consuming and, beyond recruitment, can seem ineffective or toothless without also having powers to dismiss or to override competing time commitments. But, like its seat-racing equivalent in crew selection, it brings us closest to answering that most complex of team questions: how people affect those around them and how they are influenced by them in turn.

Pursuing our quest of understanding the dynamics of relationships among high-performing individuals in the context of a team, in the next chapter we take up the effects on performance of competition and harmony within teams.

3

Why Harmony Can
Hurt Performance

The Old: Without internal harmony, teams will
                   underperform.

The New: Without internal competition, teams may
                   underperform.

The Challenge: How to manage tensions in teams
                   productively and maintain that delicate
                   balance between internal competition and
                   harmony.

Basketball stars Magic Johnson and Larry Bird once viewed contests against each other as far more significant than games against other teams, their relative levels of accomplishment being a daily preoccupation. "When the new schedule would come out each year, I'd grab it and circle the Boston games," Magic Johnson declared. "To me, it was The Two and the other 80." Similarly,

Boston Celtics' Larry Bird admitted: "The first thing I would do every morning was look at the box scores to see what Magic did. I didn't care about anything else."[1] That they respected each other's capabilities deeply is evident from each having selected the other in a fictional "perfect team" experiment of the NBA's devising.[2] But in reality too, they acknowledged each other's preeminence. During the warm-up to Bird's retirement ceremony, for example, Johnson took off his Lakers jersey to reveal a Celtics one underneath, upon which Bird replied, in jest, "Magic, get outta my dreams!" Johnson, in turn, had Bird present him at his Hall of Fame induction.[3] Competition between teams, and between star athletes on opposing teams, is good for business; coaches, managers, vendors, and the media alike exploit it. Besides, the closer teams are in terms of performance, the less predictable the outcome and the higher the gate receipts.

Competition Within Teams

But what about competition *within* teams? Jack Denfeld Wood's study of the New Haven Nighthawks ice hockey team nicely illustrates a system designed to exploit the tension between competition and cooperation within a team. Wood points out that even though hockey is a team sport, at this level it is very much an individual pursuit. The Nighthawks played in the American Hockey League, sandwiched between the top-tier National Hockey League and third-tier International Hockey League. They were effectively a farm team for the Los Angeles Kings, providing the Kings with a pool of talent from which they could draw promising players, and to which they could relegate their injured and those past their sell-by date. In practical terms, this meant that players were constantly moving, either upward by joining the premier Los Angeles team or downward to the IHL. What was good for the Kings (the development of talent) was bad for the Nighthawks (seeing their best players swapped for injured or disgruntled ones).

The system was brutally effective yet fueled interpersonal tensions: players never quite knew from day to day who would be moving where, who would stick around, or who would disappear altogether. They were aware that the primary competition was with each other for promotion to the NHL. On any given day, whether a team won or lost was far less important than a player's individual performance during the match. Players were contracted on an individual basis (with large differences in salary), and management decided on their advancement or relegation based on individual performance. The result was a complex arrangement of cooperation and competition, where the latter seems to have had the upper hand.[4]

Other team sports use similar techniques—think of soccer, basketball, and rugby, for example—where coaches select players for every match based on mock games that pit teammates against each other on the playing field. John Eales, a double world champion who captained the Australian national rugby union team a record fifty-five times, likens this to a "moveable feast": the choice of whoever appears on the field on the day of the game depends on team members' individual performances during that week's training and in recent matches.

This combinatorial game, and the internal competition it fuels, is just as acute in rowing, where the likelihood of selection hinges directly on the athletes' ability to coordinate with the very same people they compete against. Their best chance of making the cut requires them to "make for a fast boat" by creating a platform for others to also be the best they can be. Sportswriter

David Halberstam described these extraordinary pressures well: "If rowing was an estimable sport filled with virtue and honor and strength, then there was something about the team camps that was the reverse of that. They became its Darwinian lowest common denominator. This camp was, if anything, worse; it was filled with anxiety and tension that turned inevitably into paranoia. So much depended on so little that was quantifiable."[5]

For those caught on the inside, the experience can be one of acute anxiety. A reflective monologue by Jake Cornelius contains a neat example of just how acute. As a member of the U.S. Rowing squad (in preparation for the 2012 Games), Cornelius won a seat on Stanford University's varsity crew and competed in the Oxford and Cambridge Boat Race. Ashen-haired, good-looking, and six-foot-four, he arrived in Cambridge in September 2006 on the back of a 5:55 erg score (the gold standard is 6 minutes for a 2,000-meter erg test, putting Cornelius easily within the top five Cambridge oarsmen in terms of power).

Unlike many of his fellow Cambridge oarsmen, Cornelius had grown up in modest circumstances in upstate New York. The damp basement of his family's house had never been renovated, yet became Jake's bedroom and de facto gym. His first piece of equipment consisted of two paint buckets suspended on each end of a broomstick. He won his first-ever indoor rowing competition and was immediately invited to apply for Stanford's crew program (from which he graduated with a near-perfect grade-point average).

His darkest hours, documented here, provide a rare window into sport's inner game. He had just lost all of his seat races on the most important selection day of the year and was left to compete with Oli de Groot and Colin Scott for the last remaining seat in the Blue Boat.

One of the worst thoughts is that once you know what you need to do to get back on track to make the Blue Boat, it would be incredibly tough mentally as well as physically—mentally because it meant I had to ask myself all sorts of questions like "Can I really do this?" and "How good am I really?" and "What am I worth?"—and did I really want the answers to these questions? What if I were to discover that I wasn't good enough, is that something I could live with? And it's so much harder to show everything you've got and put all your cards on the table than to say fuck this, and I don't really care—but then you have to admit to yourself that you do care, that you care very much, and that's probably the biggest hurdle . . . And then seeing the guys again after [seat racing] was really tough—particularly when you know that everyone talks about you behind your back and everyone's watching to see how you will respond—and you know people are saying things about you—and I felt a lot of animosity towards the guys and to [the chief coach] in particular because it's hard to try and believe in yourself if no one else is believing in you. I knew I had given them every reason to think that I couldn't do it, but it fills you with anger to look around at each of your team-mates and think you probably don't think I can do it . . . and you don't think I can do it either . . . and you don't think I can do it—and even though they were all making a rational call based on the evidence, the only way I could respond was by saying fuck you, you don't know me—and I was also angry because I felt [the coaches] should have spotted my technical faults earlier and helped me to avoid all this bullshit—I was so embarrassed—and so I made myself a MP3 recording—

Nobody can work like I can
I have seen things they've not seen,
And done things they've not done,
And that makes me stronger

I beat Cal and Washington
Because I worked for four years
I will beat Colin and Oli
Because I will work for the next four weeks

I'm faster than Oli
I'm faster than Colin
I'm stronger than them
I work harder than them
I catch quicker
I pull harder
I move boats better than they do
I'm the fastest and the strongest

My catches are the quickest on the team
I'm the strongest rower alive
I win because I work the hardest
I get better every day and I learn faster than anybody else

I sit in the Blue Boat because I make them move faster
I am ruthless in my preparation
I work harder than anybody else
I get better faster than anybody else
I enjoy the pain and satisfaction of pushing myself to the limit

I am a tough, determined and persistent competitor
Who refuses to give in no matter how difficult the situation
I am calm and composed under pressure
And totally committed to making the Blue Boat
I know that I'm preparing for the moment I can claim my seat
And I know that I will be ready when it comes

And I decided to focus on showing the chief coach and Blue Boat how good I could be. The way I viewed it, it wasn't really a matter of who was the better oarsman between Colin, Oli and me—all that mattered was who was perceived to be better—and so I spent a lot of time thinking of how others would perceive me and I became overly sensitive to how I thought people saw me, particularly the coaches, of how they thought I compared to Colin and Oli, and I sort of knew it helped that I was taller than either of them and I looked more like the natural oarsman; and I particularly wanted the coaches to see me working hard because if you're the guy when they walk into the boathouse and see you working, it gives them the impression that you work continuously.

And so I also desperately wanted the guys in the Blue Boat to see that I was working hard, but at the same time I didn't want Colin and Oli to see me working hard because then they might start working hard too, and I didn't want them to find out until it was too late, and so they wouldn't feel threatened until it was time to threaten them on the river, though I did feel badly about this because I like Colin and Oli and feel sad about having to compete with them for a place in the Blue Boat, Oli especially as we were really good friends at the beginning of the season, whereas now it's tough to act normal around him when I've spent so much time targeting him as the guy I have to beat . . .

The fact that they were my friends meant that I knew things about them that could be perceived as insecurities that could work to my advantage, but I really didn't want to exploit them—I mean even in my own thoughts—but the mind games that I played with myself were so intense and I wanted so badly to get inside their heads and let them know

I was the alpha male; it's so confusing to mentally attack your friends—it drives you insane—but sanity seemed like a small price to pay for something I wanted so badly.[6]

Few organizations pit colleagues against each other in quite the same fashion. And yet there is often a real sense in which colleagues pitching for a contract or creating a game or new piece of software do compete for access to resources, promotions, status, or a share of the bonus pot. Rivalry within teams is particularly acute in the large professional service firms where career paths are relatively structured, from admission as a trainee to making partner. The final hurdle is by far the most challenging, where you get to share in the partnership's profits and enjoy the equity that is generated. There will be many candidates from different service functions who are encouraged to work together in their progression through the ranks knowing that the selection process for partner admission is highly competitive, with a high probability that a colleague will take one of the prized partnership slots first. Jack Welch was famously defensive of the rivalry his forced ranking had generated within General Electric. Rumor has it that a group of consultants, when expressing an interest in dismantling his rank-and-yank system, were cautioned in no uncertain terms not to mess with "my system"; Welch had worked hard to get this level of competition between top managers and was loath to see it ruined.

Competition's Consequences

Such internal competition can easily make a team feel dysfunctional, even if it is anything but. A healthy level of internal competition can help get the best out of high performers. To try to suppress any competitive element may do the team a great disservice. As Timothy Gallwey explains in *The Inner Game of Tennis*, competition and cooperation are closely intertwined. In tennis, each player tries his hardest to defeat the other, yet not for the sake of beating another player, but merely to overcome the obstacle he now presents. Thus, both players benefit by their efforts to overcome the obstacles presented by the other, both growing stronger in the process, each participating in the development of the other.[7]

Moreover, in a team context, to root out interpersonal competition in the interest of harmony may generate some unintended and quite harmful consequences. Nancy Katz, until recently on the faculty of the Harvard Kennedy School of Government, is clear about the risks of stifling competition for the sake of promoting interpersonal harmony. Rivalries, her research suggests, do not miraculously vanish. Instead, they go underground, meaning that team members begin to compete by manipulation or by belittling or even sabotaging the efforts of those around them.[8] For them, the need to compete is as innate as the need for nourishment.

Michael Jordan, arguably one of the all-time greatest athletes on the most successful basketball team of the 1990s, made no secret of his competitive streak. It was, to him, the wood that fueled the fire. He famously snubbed those who had passed him over in his formative years in his divisive Hall of Fame induction speech—the high school coach who didn't put him on the varsity team his sophomore year, his college roommate who did make the team, the NBA vets who froze him out in his first All-Star Game, and former Chicago Bulls general manager Jerry Krause.

Plus, if you need to make tough choices, you may not want your team to end up as a congenial, comfortable setting.[9] As Harvard psychologist Richard Hackman points out: "A leader can't value harmonious relationships more than putting the conditions in place that will allow the team to do well."[10] And yet the desire to work in a comfortable setting is powerful and can lead managers to bend over backward to avoid conflict, and team members to self-censor for fear of disrupting team harmony. In his own work with symphony orchestras, Hackman discovered that grumpy orchestras play together better than happy ones.[11] Who would have thought?

It is a viewpoint I subscribe to. But it does seem at odds with some relatively influential popular viewpoints, including that of Daniel Goleman, author of *Emotional Intelligence*. Goleman leaves little to the imagination when it comes to the importance of team harmony: "The ability of teams to rise to the level of star performance is determined by how harmonious the team is, how well people get along, and so on. To the extent that the people on the team feel that 'nobody cares about me,' or they are really mad at that person over there, or they can't stand the team leader, they will not contribute their best. Then they won't work well with other people; they won't be seamless in their efforts. And the actual performance of the team will be lowered directly."[12]

But what if interpersonal conflict is really the consequence, not cause, of underperforming teams? Imagine, writes Hackman, a team that has run into difficulty. It fails to live up to its promise, despite the quality of individuals on the team. It also exhibits interpersonal difficulties: conflicts between members, communication breakdowns, power struggles, and the like. What often happens is that team leaders infer that these interpersonal difficulties are causing performance problems, rather than the other way around, and that fixing the former will automatically fix the latter. As reasonable as this inference may seem, it is neither logical nor correct, for even if interpersonal difficulties can undermine performance occasionally, it simply does not follow that the best response is to help team members fix their working relationships.[13] And it is true that studies comparing task-focused interventions with those focused on improving interpersonal harmony make it abundantly clear that the task-focused variety can be far more effective in improving team performance.[14]

To demonstrate the effect of perceptions of performance on team harmony, University of California–Berkeley's Barry Staw designed a clever experiment. Using a sizable sample, he supplied teams with false feedback on their performance before asking them to provide objective descriptions of how they felt their team members had interacted with each other while performing the requisite task. Teams that were told that they had performed well, regardless of actual performance, also reported more harmonious relationships. By contrast, those who had been told their teams had underperformed were much less flattering about their teammates and far more pessimistic in evaluating the intergroup dynamics while at work. Again, their feedback had no bearing whatsoever on actual performance.[15]

Former San Francisco 49ers head coach, Bill Walsh, thinks the emphasis placed on harmony over task is particularly treacherous for those in charge: "The [best] coaches . . . know that the job is to win . . . know that they must be decisive, that they must phase people through their organizations, and at the same time they are sensitive to the feelings, loyalties, and emotions that people have toward one another. If you don't have these feelings, I do not know how you can lead anyone. I have spent many sleepless nights trying to figure out how I was going to phase out certain players for whom I had strong feelings, but that was my job. I wasn't hired to do anything but win."[16]

Team members, of course, need not be kindred spirits in order to respect or even trust each other. Put together a dozen players, several coaches, and a general manager and you'll invariably find that they won't all like each other. And perhaps that doesn't matter so long as each can rely on the other, thinks BBC football pundit,

Alan Hansen.[17] Ex-Wimbledon soccer manager Dave Bassett adds a similar comment: "We had a great team spirit, but not all the players got along. Lawrie Sanchez and John Fashanu didn't fancy each other much—they didn't get on at all in fact—but that didn't mean they wouldn't pass to each other or pull together when they were out on the pitch."[18] David Halberstam speaks of respect arising as a result of everyone, adversaries included, having subjected himself to the same cruel regime, and being left with no choice but to respect others as much as he respected himself.[19]

A Bold Experiment

But what if a team doesn't even trust in each other's abilities? An extraordinary experiment designed to mend an underperforming team by raising levels of mutual respect took place in May 2002 at the United States Military Academy. In the lead-up to the national rowing championships, Colonel Stas Preczewski, head coach of the U.S. Army Crew, faced a serious dilemma. Although Preczewski had based his selection of the top-tier (varsity) and second-tier (junior varsity) crew on carefully analyzed, objective individual performance data, the junior varsity crew kept beating the higher-status squad members two out of every three practice races on the water. Needless to say, this left the varsity crew increasingly insecure. On paper, they should have had far more power and technical prowess on board. Yet they were unable to collectively translate paper-based skills into boat speed. The more insecure they became, the more difficult it was to synchronize their strokes, and the slower the speed of their boat. This, in turn, led to the risk they would be beaten yet again. Defeat at the hands of the junior varsity did little to establish trust within the varsity crew, leading instead to plenty of finger-pointing. Consider, for example, one of several e-mails Coach Preczewski received at the time:

Now . . . my bitching session about Jim since I haven't gotten a chance to talk with you. Besides his "great personality" (which I won't even get into) he is not consistent at all and I don't know if you can tell this from outside the boat. It doesn't seem like he listens to the coxswain very well and he doesn't listen to me either. I really need someone that I feel a bond with and it isn't happening with Jim. At points I have almost asked you to move me to any boat but the one that he is in. I know and try to remember the story that you always tell about the guy that decked the other guy at the season's end, but I seriously don't think that I can hold out that long. He gets on my nerves so bad (which is odd cause I really get along with everyone) and I think everyone is starting to notice what an ass he's making out of himself and asking why he is sitting in that seat. I'm very sorry if it seems like I'm trying to get you to change something that you don't want to (because you are the coach) but I'm just trying to give you perspective from my seat.[20]

Preczewski's solution was ingenious. Realizing that all of his oarsmen had been trained in physical combat, including in wrestling and hand-to-hand combat techniques, he had his varsity crew form four pairs, matching port (or bow) side with starboard (or stroke) side. He then told them to wrestle each other for ninety seconds, before swapping them for another round. As he explained:

I told them they could wrestle each other as physically as they wanted to, as hard as they wanted to. They looked at me like I was nuts, and they didn't want to do it. I told them if they didn't do it they were cut. I immediately started wondering if my career as an officer was going to be over. People would literally pick others up and throw them onto the ground. I began thinking, how am I going to explain broken bones or skull fractures? And when I blew the whistle after 90 seconds, I had to blow it several times to get them to stop. It was ugly. They were really straining. Somewhere after the sixth or seventh match, all of a sudden there started to be some laughter from the groups. And on the next-to-last one, all of a sudden they just started all wrestling each other and jumping on each other. It was like a pile of humanity there in front of me. Just laughing and throwing one another, and suddenly it turned to hugging. It was just amazing. After the last set, which was more play than wrestling, I said "All right, go get into the boat. Hands on . . . and they went out. They had what they described as the best practice they ever had. They just flew down the Hudson. When the practice was over, they packed up the boat and sent it to the Nationals competition in Philadelphia. At Nationals, they had their heat-race on Friday and placed second, which put them into the semifinals. On Saturday morning they placed second in the semifinals. This was the best performance that any Army Crew had ever had. Their time was far better than the JV boat, and the JV boat took a bronze medal in their own event. They all walked home happy.[21]

Preczewski's decision was courageous, given the risk of injury involved in a wrestling match so close to the Nationals. But it worked wonders in restoring a sense of trust within the crew—confidence in the sheer power that each of the oarsmen was able to bring to the crew, as well as in each other's determination to make a fast boat.

Competition and Collaboration

Team-oriented skills that do not always have priority over individual performance measures amplify the uncomfortable relation between rivalry and collaboration within teams. Take such team-focused actions as rebounds, blocked shots, assists, and steals in basketball as a case in point. Ironically, they are far poorer predictors of the player's amount of playing time than such individualistic measures as ability to score, based on NBA draft data, making it difficult for players to be team players.[22] In fact, there are few, if any, statistics a basketball player accumulates that cannot be amassed selfishly. As Daryl Morey, general manager of the Houston Rockets, put it: "We think about this deeply whenever we're talking about contractual incentives. We don't want to incent a guy to do things that hurt the team" and, adds author Michael Lewis, "the amazing thing about basketball is how easy this is to do."[23]

In corporate life, too, incentive schemes often prioritize individual over collective achievement, and striking the right balance can be difficult to achieve. Shortly after his arrival in early 2002, Nick Wilkinson, as managing director of Dixons Retail, one of the largest consumer electronics retailers in Europe, actively tried to combine an already high level of internal competition by adding a team reward. As a consequence, many of his best salespeople left, discouraged by what they felt was a system intent on watering down their individual contributions. According to Wilkinson, "The I in team is important but there's no scope here for people that are only ever I, meaning it's always about them and them alone, and everyone else can go to hell."[24] However, to cater to the spirit of competition that is part of the young recruits eager to progress up the career ladder, he designed a plan in which stores were encouraged to compete against other Dixons stores of a similar size but in a different region. He also encouraged recruits to be transparent about their career ambitions via an internal, online application system. Everyone had access to whatever anyone else was planning as a career. Internal competition wasn't so much eradicated as reoriented: some of it toward other stores, and some of it channeled toward career development rather than competition for the next customer.

A rather less successful example involves Xerox, which divided its technicians into three groups as part of a new experiment. It paid the first group individually; the second received team-based compensation; and the third, a mixture of both. Researchers used the experiment to tease out the effects of the various compensation packages. The group with the worst performance result had the mixed compensation. Its members were not told what proportion of their pay was team-based and what was based on individual performance. As a result, they were terribly confused about how to divide their time between individual- and team-based activities.[25]

General Electric's rank-and-yank approach, referred to earlier, lavishly rewards top performers while routinely letting go the bottom 10 percent. One predictable consequence of GE's approach has been to drive individuals to high performance but, where necessary, at the expense of others on their teams. For example, given the premium placed on information, individuals revealed their ideas only at high-profile meetings in order to maximize the impact for them as individuals. To get the balance between competition and collaboration right is one of the most difficult team-leadership challenges.

Trust and Vigilance

Competition and cooperation are not the only sources of tension in high-performance teams. There are others: trust and vigilance, control and autonomy, confrontation and compromise, creativity and protocol, stability and change, democratic and autocratic decision making, the pros and cons of working in silos, the development of the individual and of others. The latter is typically high on the list at professional service firms, which rank individuals based on their billing performance. To develop associates into partnership candidates requires time and resources, and yet isn't easily billable. The silo mentality that is often a frequent source of complaint in professional service firms—it limits valuable cross-selling of products—can provide a strong sense of identity and social cohesion.

Then again, as many professional service firms have discovered to their demise, clients can quickly commoditize services delivered from these silos, and the only way to combat commoditization is to merge siloed skills to produce tailored solutions. Moreover, the firms' inability or unwillingness to cross-sell services or cross-pollinate may leave substantial amounts of money on the table. Take Sony and DaimlerChrysler, for example. Each proved unable to get its internal divisions to collaborate effectively, so Sony could not come up with its own version of the iPod or iTunes, and DaimlerChrysler had to dismantle its joint operations at a loss of some $35 billion. Microsoft too had apparently developed a viable tablet computer over a decade earlier but failed to preempt Apple's iPad because, says a former company executive, internal divisions had conspired to kill the project.[26]

Likewise, trust and vigilance coexist in varying degrees, as trust comes in different guises. For instance, it could signify confidence in team members' technical competence, in their reliability, or in their benevolence. In much research on trust, the concept remains relatively poorly defined and referring to some combination of these three varieties, making it difficult to pin down. Nevertheless, some researchers exploring the topic of trust in teams have offered interesting suggestions. Penn State professor Kimberly

Merriman, for example, thinks that low-trust teams are best rewarded according to individual effort. The fact that an estimated 85 percent of Fortune 1,000 companies use some form of team or group-based pay would thus suggest that they either think their teams have transcended the low-trust barrier or hope that pay might promote trust. If the latter is true, it seems ironic that cooperation is far better fostered by shared perceptions of fairness, of which the allocation of specific roles and individualized rewards are key features.[27]

Evidence from NCAA basketball suggests that, when it comes to team performance, trust placed in coaches is more important than that among teammates. Survey results from thirty college basketball teams (eleven from Division I and nineteen from Division III), drawn from twelve conferences, show a distinct relationship between high levels of trust in the coach and performance insofar as trust in leadership allows players to suspend their questions, doubts, and personal motives and instead fully participate in whatever the team is required to do. Of course, the difficulty with this type of research is that of causal direction: is it trust in the coach that helps performance or the other way around?[28]

Either way, more trust isn't necessarily better. One can have too much of a good thing. A recent experiment with teams of executive MBA students given two hundred colored-plastic bricks (from which they were asked to craft nothing more sophisticated than a coat stand) finds that trust can be the death knell to creativity. While trust is associated with creativity—not least because it signifies a psychologically safe space in which people can tinker freely without fear of losing face—this really only applies up to a point. Beyond this, trust becomes a liability. Team members placed a higher premium on harmony than on solving the problem at hand. The creative tension that results from questioning each other's suggestions gives way to trying to please one another.[29]

Researchers drew similar conclusions from a sample of seventy-one self-managed teams of MBA students, where high trust correlated positively with high performance so long as individual autonomy remained low. Where trust between teammates resulted in them having more control over their own fiefdoms, performance took a nosedive. The implication is that teammates should trust but be vigilant, even as excessive amounts of vigilance inevitably risk eroding whatever trust relationship they have cultivated.[30]

Control and Autonomy, Stability and Change

Similar tension exists between control and autonomy, where the efficiency-enhancing function of control can be compromised by empowering those less experienced, even though giving them free rein may be the best way for them to learn on the job. Besides, empowerment has been found to be positively correlated with both team performance and satisfaction.[31] But to emphasize one invariably comes at the expense of the other.

The same is true with forces for change and stability. Change can be refreshing: new faces help cast new perspectives on old problems. As David Bolchover and Chris Brady note in their analysis of British soccer managers, the best of them periodically renew their teams. They do so to reassure themselves that their team will have the necessary skills and resources to face new, possibly tougher challenges. The authors give the example of Brian Clough, immortalized in the movie *The Damned United*, who was forced to make some tough choices when his team, Nottingham Forest was promoted to the First Division in 1977. Clough was keenly aware that his current team was not good enough to survive in soccer's top division without reinforcements and, within a month of the start of the new season, had purchased three players of proven quality: Peter Shilton, Kenny Burns, and Archie Gemmill. Nottingham Forest came from nowhere to win the League Championship that season.[32] Even Manchester United's Sir Alex Ferguson has continued to rejuvenate what is still one of the most successful clubs in English soccer by adding new players, even during winning seasons, including Roy Keane, Andy Cole, and Ronnie Johnsen and Ole Gunnar Solskjaer.[33]

Yet team stability is important, too. Sir Alex may have added new players when he felt they would improve the club's performance but he is eager to emphasize the importance of longevity, too. Bringing to mind such players as Peter Schmeichel, Steve Bruce, and Garry Pallister, he noted that "the longer players are here, it becomes a natural progression of the way the club has been over the last 15 years. It has its qualities. It has a fantastic profile, history and a good philosophy in the way they play the game. They have had winning qualities going back all these years and that is why they are dominant now."[34]

When it comes to the importance of stability, evidence from the airline industry is compelling as well. A U.S. National Transportation Safety Board investigation in 1994 discovered that 73 percent of all in-flight incidents occur on the first day a particular flight crew works together. When NASA's Ames Research Center decided to extend this finding in a subsequent experimental simulation, it concluded that fatigued flight crews or those that had already flown together for several days caught and corrected more errors than did well-rested crews just starting out, having not previously collaborated.[35] In a corporate world preoccupied with change, it is easy to forget the merits of the stability provided by individuals working together for prolonged periods of time. Here too, striking the balance between renewal and continuity is one of leadership's most challenging tasks.

Greed and Altruism

Somewhat subtler is the tension between greediness and altruism among team members. Intuition tells us that selfless individuals should be popular; after all, they give a lot to the team yet ask little in return. It is equally obvious that selfish behavior is undesirable: if people were into it solely for themselves, they might free ride if given the chance, leaving some tasks either undone or poorly done. Here, the selfless might pick up the pieces and compensate for others. However, a surprising finding from recent experiments proves intuition wrong. Who would have thought that team members value charitable individuals much less than we (or even they) might expect.

Psychologists Craig Parks and Asako Stone came to this entirely unexpected finding after an experiment designed to study the expected ostracism of cheaters. Early results showed that team members were as likely to select the generous minded for exclusion. Using a computer simulation of a simple game, participants were given ten points per round to keep or place in a "public goods" kitty. Whatever points they put in the shared pool would double, after which participants could withdraw up to 25 percent of the pool (irrespective of their original investment). There was an incentive to withdraw less than 25 percent, namely, a bonus would be paid if the pool exceeded a certain threshold after an unspecified number of rounds. After the game, the psychologists asked the participants which of four players (one of whom was either a Scrooge or a martyr) they would like to play in another round. Unsurprisingly, the selfish person proved unpopular, but so did the selfless. So bewildering was the result that they reran the experiment four times while simultaneously testing alternative explanations.

67

So why is it that people are as likely to exclude selfless people as those who are greedy? Might it be that people are inherently bad at correctly estimating the contributions of those around them? So, if you take a smaller share, it reflects on you as having given less in the first place. Or, similarly, if you take less than others, this indicates the value you place on your own contribution, meaning that if you don't value yourself, why should team members? The researchers' first explanation—that the selfless person was perceived as incompetent or unpredictable, or the kind of person psychologists know will be disliked in this sort of game—proved to be false. When questioned, participants reported that seeing others take less than their fair share made them feel bad, and that the only way to rescue their own reputations (and make themselves feel better by comparison) was to eliminate the martyr. Virtue had become vice.[36]

Tensions Ignite Outstanding Individual Performance

These seemingly contradictory forces coexist, in a perfectly natural way. Competition weeds out inefficiency in an otherwise collaborative environment. Trust can lower transaction costs but also lead to free riding if not paired with some degree of vigilance. Control can prevent waste, particularly when dealing with less experienced team members, yet autonomy is what allows them to make mistakes and learn from them, or to handle difficulties with clients they know well rather than those more senior but also more detached. Charisma can become manipulative if those who are more analytical do not rein it in. Analysis without charisma can fuel cynicism. Patience is a virtue but, if too widely shared, could cause a team to be indecisive; hence it helps to have someone on board who is more decisive, even if being too decisive can lead to hasty choices. Granting colleagues autonomy provides scope for personal growth and flexibility, yet too much autonomy enables them to build their own empires. This means that control is required, although too much control can be seen as autocratic, off-putting, and ineffective. Open-mindedness allows for flexibility and creativity, but too much of it can render teams indiscriminate. Loyalty to key ideas, to ground rules, or to those in charge might balance that out, but loyalty that is too strong can cause teams to miss opportunities.

These tensions can quite easily make a team of high performers seem fragile, even if it is perfectly functional. The tensions can make even the most effective teams feel off-balance occasionally, as teammates work to reconcile, or reconcile themselves, to the contrary pulls. The potential for conflict is never far away, not just because those team members often fall prey to their own insecurities, but because they believe things should be done in particular ways.

Orson Welles, as Harry Lime in a film version of Graham Greene's novel *The Third Man,* makes much the same point: "In Italy, for 30 years under the Borgias, they had warfare, terror, murder, and bloodshed, but they produced Michelangelo, Leonardo da Vinci, and the Renaissance. In Switzerland, they had brotherly love. They had 500 years of democracy and peace, and what did that produce? The cuckoo clock."[37] Welles's declaration—or, more precisely, that of the scriptwriter—is insightful, even if wrong in at least one matter of detail: the cuckoo clock was invented in Bavaria, Germany. But the point is clear: what feels dysfunctional need not be. Tension may be unpleasant but not therefore illegitimate and necessary to eradicate.

How then can we help teams, whether at work or in sports, in the boardroom or in the pool, manage discomfort constructively? We will turn to this issue in the next chapter.

4

Why Perception Matters More Than Reality

The Old:	Everyone needs to be on the same page.
The New:	People have different versions of reality. Whether they are correct is less relevant than what their realities tell you about their priorities.
The Challenge:	How to manage conflict constructively.

It is not difficult to see why conflict within teams is inevitable. High performers inhabit a world of contradictory forces, where success often hinges on outperforming their teammates, or the very people they rely on for moral support, in a world where small margins make big differences. High performers are likely to overestimate their own contributions and uniqueness, as noted in chapter 1. Their behavior is calculated, and, given high stakes and the realization that objective criteria alone do not drive promotions, they can be prone to paranoia. As a consequence, what often inflames an otherwise harmless if unpleasant quarrel is the default response it generates. Particularly when faced with promotion pressures or ongoing competition for status individuals query the intentions of those around them. Yet few things are more alienating or offensive than a person's intentions being called into question. Thus, the real irony of team conflict is that it tends to arise even though the intentions of those on the team are actually benign, meaning that those involved agree to a common purpose and actually try hard to align their efforts with teammates.

The preparations of Bobby Fischer and his support team for the 1972 World Chess Championship match against Boris Spassky provide a poignant illustration of just such paranoia. Having won his first U.S. chess championship at age fourteen, Fischer, then twenty-nine, was about to face his fiercest challenger. It was a highly anticipated event. Prize money was set at an unprecedented $78,125 for the winner, $46,975 for the loser, and a thick slice of television and film profits. Some one hundred fifty newspaper reporters from thirty-two countries arrived in Iceland to relay the event to the world as it unfolded.

The problem was that Fischer hadn't yet arrived. He had been suspicious of Iceland as the match venue ever since finding out it had been Spassky's first choice for a site. He suspected Max Euwe, the president of the organizing committee, to be a "tool for the Russians," and his U.S. mentor, Ed Edmondson, of having betrayed him to the Russians in a private negotiation. He even accused the U.S. government of agreeing to sidetrack the match to Iceland in order to entomb any defeat safely away from either of the Cold War factions. Fischer eventually was persuaded to board the plane to Iceland, but not after dragging his support team through living hell.[1]

A much less innocuous example involved the decision by the 2007 coaching team of the Cambridge University Boat Club to swap the seating positions of its world champion stroke Thorsten Engelmann and its Olympic gold medalist Kieran West only nine days before the big race. The coaches had sold their decision to the crew as a temporary, two-outing measure to allow Engelmann to feel the boat's rhythm further down the boat. However, no sooner did the coaches retain West at stroke for a third outing, than the crew promptly accused them of plotting to keep him in the stroke seat for the race. Stroke is rowing's most prestigious seat in setting the rating and rowing pattern for the crew.

Tom James, as club president, called for an urgent meeting, and, as the guys gathered on the upstairs floor of a rented boathouse on the Welsh border, West himself offered to resume his less prestigious, former seat:

> For goodness' sake, it really isn't just up to stroke to set the boat rhythm; it's up to each and every one of us, so at the end of the day it makes bugger all difference whether Thorsten or I sit at the front. We have all got to take collective responsibility for the boat moving together so please let's stop messing about and wasting time worrying about who sits where and concentrate on what we can each do to influence the boat speed. That applies to everyone equally: me, Thorsten, Pete, Tom, whoever ... So Thorsten sits at stroke, I'm at Six, we all stop worrying about what everyone else is doing and bloody well concentrate on our individual jobs. That way we'll win this bloody race and none of this will matter. Problem solved![2]

The coaches were never given a chance to make any closing statements at the meeting, even though their intentions had been perfectly benign all along and fairly well aligned with those of the oarsmen. Nor were they any longer expected to make any decisions. The crewmen had effectively taken things into their own hands. The boat belonged to them.

Competing Versions of the Truth

What often lies at the core of these types of conflict are different opinions for why things are the way they are and not otherwise. Team life is, of course, replete with the giving and receiving of explanations: Why was Fischer's chess match slated to be played in Iceland? Why was West kept in stroke seat for three consecutive outings? Why did Roy Hodgson stand down from his position as team manager of Liverpool Football Club? Why did the Chicago Cubs part with 2010 Pitcher of the Year Chris Archer?

Giving, receiving, and evaluating explanations are important features of the workplace, too. Why did Bob from accounting resign? Why did Lehman Brothers really collapse? We typically respond to questions like these by providing explanations about possible causes. Arguments develop around whether these causal explanations are likely to be right or wrong. There is, after all, a premium on getting them right, since they inform our decisions on what we might do differently next time. Yet while we accept that contrasting explanations are part and parcel of human experience, they can escalate cognitive conflict into relational conflict. Whereas the former can be helpful, the latter is corrosive. To effectively defuse relational conflict requires us to appreciate that contrasting explanations are much less about *what happened* than about *what matters*.

Cricketer Ed Smith supplies some helpful examples of how sports fans can generate vastly different explanations for successes and failures.[3] Using the case of England's 2005 Ashes win, he asks whose victory it really was. Was it destiny, strategy, luck, the coaches, or the players? And if so who specifically? As Smith explains:

> According to former England skipper Nasser Hussain it was down to the coach, Duncan Fletcher. Chris Adams, captain of Sussex, felt England's resurgence owed much to the improved standard of county cricket. To students of physics and mechanics, the answer lay in the mysterious business of reverse swing. To arch-skeptics, it was pure luck: Australia were in a dominant position in the Ashes until Glenn McGrath suffered a freak ankle injury just before the start of the second Test. More generous spirits believed in the power of leadership—the Ashes belong to Michael Vaughan. To the many men on the street, it was simpler still: England had a true hero again, a man called Andrew Flintoff.[4]

Smith, also a history graduate from Cambridge, makes the point that in history, as in everyday life, people often disagree about the past. In the context of sports and business, in particular, the explanations they give for what may or may not have taken place tend to be future oriented. So, college basketball fans are concerned with making the Sweet 16; ice hockey fans, the Stanley Cup Final; baseball fans, the World Series; football fans, the Super Bowl; soccer fans, European Cup Finals; and everyone else, with winning the next match. They tend to leave nostalgia to the television commentators for fear of succumbing to its paralyzing effects. The problem, Smith thinks, is fourfold. The simplest is that people easily forget: "Professional sports is a relentless cycle of journeys, practice sessions, team-talks and matches. Motorways merge in the mind. Hotel foyers blur in the memory. Bags are constantly packed, unpacked, left behind. Forms are signed, bills paid. The road is as much home as home itself. Flux disorientates; pressure numbs; memories fray."[5] Corporate life is often no different. One meeting room is pretty much like another, and there is little to distinguish hotels, gyms, lounges, or limousines. In fact, even if there were differences, they would quickly be obliterated by perpetual fatigue and eyestrain that drag from one time zone into the next. Hence, it is hardly surprising that people's accurate recollection of past events can be less than useful.

Occasionally, people remember some but not all facts. Or they correctly recall relevant facts but interpret them wrongly. As former England's cricket coach, Duncan Fletcher, writes in *Ashes Regained*, Michael Vaughan's lack of runs scored at the start of the 2005 season was often explained by his moving too much before the cricket ball was bowled.[6] Not true, says Fletcher. Vaughan, at bat, was moving just as much in 2005 as he had in previous seasons, the exception being that the timing of his movements was better. In other words, his movements were so carefully synchronized with the ball's arrival that they created the illusion of stillness.

From time to time, people fall prey to the fallacy of inevitability or the belief that success or failure was somehow meant to be. In doing so, they bypass any attempt at mapping out cause and effect by reverting to grand narratives instead (e.g., "our time had come") or overly simplistic explanations (e.g., "Jack's recent divorce caused him to take his eye off the ball during the vital ninth inning with all bases loaded and two outs"). Explanations of business success and failure are often no better. People easily resort to heroism (e.g., Jack Welch at GE), luck (e.g., Pfizer's Viagra), or inevitability (e.g., the meltdown of the financial system), depending on who is doing the explaining. The wide acceptance of such explanations in business is curious because, as in sports, accurate explanations ought to be highly prized, assuming that they inform future decisions.

Popular narrative can easily trump brute fact. A fascinating example from medical history entails nineteenth-century physician, Ignaz Semmelweis, and his preoccupation with the high incidence of maternal and child mortality due to puerperal fever in a ward of Vienna General Hospital. Noticing that the occurrence of fever was substantially higher in wards where the same doctors also conducted postmortems, he suggested they should wash their hands with a chlorinated lime solution after working on cadavers. Alas, fact didn't fit narrative: at the time, people believed health to be a function of balance between four humors of the human body. To suggest that lack of cleanliness on the part of the physicians was to blame for the mortality rates was considered insulting. Doctors summarily dismissed Semmelweis's findings and did not take them seriously until after his death on August 13, 1865.[7]

Why What Matters Is More Important Than What Happened

To get a sense of just how complex causal history can be, and the extent to which explanations are driven not just by "what matters" but by "what happened," it helps to unpack one case in some detail. The case involves a conundrum that still preoccupies some of the best minds in business schools, even though the incident itself took place some time ago. It also happens to still be one of the most popular in MBA classrooms: Honda's extraordinary success in capturing a share of the U.S. motorcycle market in the late 1950s and 1960s.[8]

By 1954, Honda had become one of Japan's leading motorcycle manufacturers. It enjoyed a solid 15 percent share of the domestic Japanese market. In 1958, it introduced a new, lightweight 50cc model called the Super Cub, which became highly popular in Japan and accounted for more than half of Honda's sales by the end of the 1950s.[9] On the back of this success, Honda began to contemplate expanding into the United States. It made the decision to go ahead in 1958, and a small advance group of Honda executives arrived in the United States in late 1959, initially with the aim of gaining a foothold in the midsized bike market. However, it was the Super Cub that attracted attention in the U.S., and that quickly became the main draw. Sales rose dramatically, from $500,000 in 1960 to $77 million in 1965, by which time Honda had captured more than 50 percent of the U.S. motorcycle market.

Various organizations have offered explanations for Honda's success over the ensuing five decades. The earliest and best known are included in a Boston Consulting Group (BCG) report delivered to the British government and Britain's ailing motorcycle industry in 1975. Richard Pascale, a former McKinsey consultant and Stanford University professor, wrote a revisionist response to BCG's account. Like most of the authors who have contributed to the debate, BCG and Pascale concentrate on what they see as key promoting causes. On the one hand, BCG presented Honda's success as the outcome of a calculated attempt to exploit economies of scale, made possible by high sales volumes in Japan and superior engineering. On the other hand, Pascale's account, based on an interview with the six executives responsible for Honda's entry into the United States, argued that Honda did not follow a carefully premeditated strategy and was expecting to make a mark with its larger motorcycles instead.

Honda, however, was initially sceptical about the prospects of the Super Cub in the United States and more concerned about developing a market for its midsized models. That the Super Cub turned out to be attractive to U.S. buyers came as a surprise, something that became apparent not because of any deliberate actions on Honda's part, but by accident when Honda noticed the favorable commentary it was attracting. As the Japanese executives explained to Pascale: "We used the Honda 50s ourselves to ride around Los Angeles on errands. They attracted a lot of attention. One day we had a call from a Sears buyer. While persisting in our refusal to sell through an intermediary, we took note of Sears' interest."[10] Honda's success with the Super Cub was primarily the result of incremental learning and luck. While the two accounts do not contradict each other in every aspect, the discrepancies were significantly stark to crystallize differences between advocates of planning and learning that continue to be debated to this day in MBA classrooms.

Any event as complex as Honda's successful entry into the U.S. motorcycle market will have a long and complicated causal history. It is thus hardly surprising that various accounts of the episode have invoked all manner of promoting causes: cost advantages in Japan; technological superiority; persistence grounded in a culture intolerant of failure; severe government constraints; preparedness, exemplified by Honda's initial advance party taking four different size bikes along with them; their location in Los Angeles, with its large population of Japanese descendents, a sunny climate, and proximity to Japan; Honda's ability to negotiate favorable terms with distributors; chance, as exemplified in a Sears buyer's discovery of a Super Cub; the role of core competencies; wider structural economic factors; and so on.

Not least among these are claims about what Honda may have believed and intended. As UCLA's Richard Rumelt put it:

> The key element in the controversy is intentionality: Did Honda knowingly and purposefully translate its early product success in Japan into high-volume, low-cost facilities? Did Honda "plan" its entry into the U.S. market? In particular, did Honda enter knowing that 50cc bikes were a "loose brick"? Did Honda anticipate the segment retreat strategies of British firms? Did Honda deliberately lose money to build share in order to generate the scale to ultimately deliver the best quality at the lowest cost? Did Honda "understand" that its competence was engine design and both expand and diversify in ways that enhanced and built upon this "core competence"?[11]

We are unlikely to ever know for sure what Honda did or did not intend when targeting the United States. As *Financial Times* columnist John Kay put it: "Even if we administered truth drugs to Honda executives, we would not learn more. Nor would we need to change the messages—understand your competitive advantages and design your distribution strategies around them—that Honda's success has for other businesses."[12] However, the case is insightful not just in exemplifying the coexistence of contrary, empirically well-founded, and reasonable explanations of what happened but in giving us a window on what *matters* from the perspective of those doing the explaining.

For example, in defending the BCG report, one of its authors, Michael Goold, explicitly cites the fact that the report was targeted at Britain's motorcycle industry and the U.K. government that commissioned it. After allowing that from a historical perspective, criticisms of the report's take on Honda's entry into the United States are "probably correct" and that the "report does not dwell on how Honda strategy was evolved and on the learning that took place." He concludes: "However, the report was commissioned for an industry in crisis, with the brief of identifying commercially viable alternatives. The perspective required was managerial ('what should we do now?'), not historical ('how did this situation arise?'). And for most executives concerned with strategic management the primary interest will always be 'what should we do now?'"[13]

In stark contrast to Goold and his BCG colleagues, Pascale had no obligation to arrive at prescriptions for the U.K. motorcycle industry. Rather, his revisionist account follows naturally from his long-standing interest in contrasting Japanese and Western management styles. Indeed, his research into Japanese-managed companies began in 1974, a good ten years earlier. His objective was to point out "managerial blind spots related to American culture and society."[14] One of the companies Pascale studied was the Honda Motor Co. He wrote his oft-cited article on the Honda effect after his influential book *The Art of Japanese Management*. He is entirely consistent with his interests in positioning the Japanese way of thinking as being centrifugal rather than centripetal, tolerant of ambiguity, peripheral in vision, and sophisticated in integrating the social and spiritual elements of everyday life into their organizations.[15]

Similarly, Henry Mintzberg's enthusiasm for Pascale's revisionist account is entirely consistent with his interests as represented in his earlier work. His book *The Nature of Managerial Work* entails a detailed study of what managers do and is a corrective to the popular view of the manager as "American genius for efficiency." The book was inspired by his PhD research, which comprised a detailed study of five chief executives at work. He explains his motivation for the study: "It never occurred to me (nor, apparently, to many of those who taught me [at MIT]) that nothing was said about the job of the manager—even though the master's program was ostensibly designed to train managers!"[16]

How to Resolve These Conflicts

In sum, in sports and business alike, explanations about "what happened" are revealing about "what matters." And it may well be this relation that allows conflict to escalate from an exchange of contrary ideas to something altogether more personal and potentially more destructive. As Ed Smith suggests, in advocating particular explanations, team members reveal what actually worries them. The distinction, subtle though it is, is crucially important to the resolution of conflict in teams. Thus, Kieran West repeatedly emphasized the importance of rhythm in generating boat speed for Cambridge. Having lost the 2006 Boat Race, his explanation blamed the crew's inability to settle into a sustainable rhythm. In his own words: "With the people we had on board we should have been able to win the race by Hammersmith, been clear ahead of Oxford, and sheltered on the Surrey station before getting to the point where the weather on Middlesex became as critical as it did. This year we've got to get the crew to settle into a rhythm in a way we were never able to achieve last year."[17]

Lack of rhythm may well have been partly to blame for the last year's loss, though other factors likely played a role as well, including the team's decision not to install water pumps in rough water conditions, whereas Oxford did, and frequent bickering within the crew throughout the training period. The point is that rhythm mattered to West, and, for the team to move forward, this had to be addressed. In this particular case, a team discussion resulted in the appointment of a new coxswain. Whether their former coxswain really was to blame for the crew's underperformance during the training season or was hung out to dry instead is less important than West's obsession with rhythm.

Dialogue, however, isn't necessarily the only or most effective way to resolve disagreement. Where quarrels are relatively benign, the better solution may be to put the team to work on a challenging task. As Harvard's Richard Hackman points out, task-oriented intervention has been shown to be more effective than intervention focused on restoring harmony by means of a conversation. However, where conflict has reached beyond the point at which a collective challenge might prove therapeutic, something quite different is called for. Given conflict's strong emotional roots, it is imperative that issues are disarmed from their emotional component as effectively as possible by creating a psychologically safe space for people to voice their anger, pain, or frustration. What is important here is that this occurs in the presence of those complicit in the conflict. People need to tell you how something you might have said or done made them feel before being able to engage rationally with the problem. The American poet Maya Angelou put it beautifully: "I've learned that people will forget what you said, people will forget what you did, but people will never forget how you made them feel." Recognizing the importance of tackling emotion first is at the core of conflict resolution.

A tried and tested approach to resolving team conflict is based on mediation principles jointly developed by Tufts, MIT, and Harvard Law School. I have used the approach in team mediations on many occasions—both in sports and as a member of the Cambridge University mediating team. It has proved remarkably effective. For the best possible chances of success, it is imperative to have sufficient, uninterrupted time and a relatively private location for the mediation. A boardroom or historically important space (such as a trophy room) will do, even a locker room, anything but a public space where people might be distracted or overheard.

At the Cambridge University Boat Club, I would begin by proposing some ground rules. These rules included: "What happens here stays here. This is no one's business but our own. This is a voluntary process that may or may not work, but it is probably the only viable option left, so let's agree to stick with it for as long as it takes. When one of you talks, everyone else agrees to listen without interrupting." I then asked, "Is this something you can agree to?" It is crucially important to get everyone's consent before beginning the mediation process.

With the Boat Club, this process involved four distinct phases. First, I asked people to say what they would wish to achieve in the session. What would be a good outcome for them personally? What about for the crew? In most cases, people will rapidly discover common ground and find broad agreement on what a good resolution might be. Second, going around the room, I asked people to tell each other how the current situation made them feel. The point here was not to explain what they thought the conflict was about, but how it affected them emotionally. The aim was to separate the emotive from the technical, matter-of-fact part of the conflict. This is often the most difficult and most time-consuming phase of the mediation, as people expressing raw emotions may feel that things are getting worse rather than better. The point was that team members let others know how they felt, acknowledging that for once they were being listened to and taken seriously.

After tackling the emotional component head on, it was now often easier to take a more matter-of-fact look at whatever technical issues were impeding progress and agree on a broad way forward. I typically ended with all team members making a specific commitment to resolve the issue and called on one individual to make a commitment in turn. So, for example, one person might have committed to being more coachable and better able to listen to suggestions from other crew members, but recognizing too that he could not solve the issue alone and needed someone else to commit to doing something in turn. The point of this last phase was to provide the crew with a take-away from the conversation and a sense of hope that tomorrow would be better than yesterday. In fact, it might not be a bad idea to follow the session with a task, game, match, or outing—as indeed we often did.

As in most walks of life, the explanations that team members provide are imperfect. They are charged with ideology, with hope and uncertainties. And they are meaningful, not as an accurate record of what happened but of what matters. At the root of much team conflict is disagreement on why things are as they are and not otherwise, which too easily escalates as colleagues begin to question each other's motives. To recognize explanations for what they are—a visceral reminder of what matters to people personally—is often a good first step to calming the waters.

Better yet, there are ways to preempt conflict by coaching individual team members to recognize and develop strategies for tackling issues that impede their progress as individuals and invariably the team's progress. One approach is rooted in the belief that individuals have priorities and loyalties above and beyond their team. Those charged with leadership should align their team's performance with organizational objectives, assuming that the organization actually matters to the individuals involved. In some cases, it no doubt does. Think of organizations focused on, for example, affirming the rights of the child; protecting rare animals, forests, or national monuments; providing disaster relief; fighting a war; or even supporting sports organizations with deep local roots.

However, I suspect that in reality many people care less than their organizations suppose. But clearly they do care about some things. Hence, to escalate collective effectiveness paradoxically involves smoking out these priorities. Assuming the team succeeds in what it needs to do, what will that give each team member personally? For example, achieving a sales target collectively may lead to career advancement that, in turn, brings money and prestige, which would allow for an extra family holiday, the pride of a spouse or partner, perhaps long-awaited acknowledgment from a parent of a wise career choice, or whatever ultimately matters at a deep personal level.

Olympic-swimmer and performance-consultant Adrian Moorhouse cites the example of a regional manager at Safeway who was trying to save £10 million in food waste. The store managers tackled this challenge in different ways: some decided on specific savings to be generated in the bakery, the meat and fish counters, and the produce department; others left it to the creativity of those running the counters. One of the store managers, Gail Fernandes, faced a predictable challenge from her baker: "What's in it for us?" Fernandes countered with the offer of a small bonus and a question of her own: "If I can get you a few hundred pounds as a shared bonus, what will that give you?" The baker, on reflection, decided the money would be best spent on a new family sofa. When Moorhouse returned to Fernandes's store a week later, the staff notice board featured a sheet of paper with cutouts from magazines of what each staff member would buy with his or her bonus money, alongside individual targets.[18]

A Systematic Approach to Constructive Conflict Management

A similar approach known as GROW (goals, reality, options, and will) uses a carefully structured series of questions. David Whitaker employed this approach in coaching the Great Britain hockey team to Olympic gold and bronze, and Olympic gold medalist David Hemery has used it for coaching British hurdlers to world-class performance. It is also a popular tool in coaching executive teams, one I've often used myself.

Developed by Graham Alexander and popularized in 1992 by Sir John Whitmore, the GROW model structures coaching conversations along the four topics of goals, reality, options, and will by posing a set of questions for each category.[19]

GOALS

- What would you be happy to achieve with this coaching session?

- What would you like to achieve in the long term?

- What are the minimum and maximum time frames that would satisfy you?

- How much personal control, or influence, do you have over this goal?

- What would be a good milestone along the way?

- What would we need to add so this goal is more worthwhile for you personally?

- What would we need to add so it is more worthwhile to the team?

- What would be an objective measure of progress? How about a subjective one?

- What should be in this goal to make it sustainable?

REALITY

- What is happening now?

- When things are going badly (as far as this issue is concerned), what is the effect on you? What is the effect on team members?

- Putting yourself in your team members' position for a moment, what do you think their experience of this situation is?

- What have you tried so far? What results did that produce?

- What is holding you back? Why?

OPTIONS

- What options do you have?

- What else could you do?

- If you could get advice from anyone, whom might that be?

- Who may have been through something similar with whom you could reflect on your position?

- If you had more time, what could you do?

- If you had less time, but still had to move forward, what could you do?

- If you were in charge, what would you do?

- What might you do if you knew you couldn't fail?

- If you had a magic wand, what would you most like to change, and why?

- What quality in you could you enhance to help you?

- What advice would you give a friend if he or she had this same issue?

- What would a really good friend who knew you and your issue intimately tell you to do?

WILL

- Which option(s) do you now choose?

- When will you do it?

- What is your first step?

- What could block your option and what can you do to ensure it doesn't?

- Who else is involved in your plan?

- What do you need those people to do for you?

- Whose support do you need?

- What will you do to obtain that support, and when?

- On a scale of one to ten, what commitment do you have in taking these actions? And what is preventing this from being a perfect ten, if it isn't?

Helping individuals in teams work through issues that relate to their own performance and that of the team overall not only helps prevent relational (as opposed to cognitive) conflict but helps people see how reliant they are on the support of fellow team members in realizing their own aspirations. As team members ask for support, interdependencies between them become transparent. Paradoxically, coaching individuals in teams is far more likely to strengthen, rather than undermine, the effective functioning of the team as a whole.

In the next chapter, we examine a perennial problem that relates to team size. Are we better off with slightly under-resourced over over-resourced teams? What really happens to individual productivity as the size of the team increases?

5

Why Productivity Tumbles with Size

The Old: Large teams become increasingly inefficient
                  as coordination becomes more difficult.
The New: Large teams become increasingly inefficient
                  as people try less hard.
The Challenge: How to eradicate social loafing.

Why do American football teams have eleven players; Canadian football, twelve; and Gaelic, fifteen? And why eleven in soccer? Why does Rugby Union have fifteen players, while Rugby League makes do with thirteen? Why does baseball field nine players; basketball, five; volleyball, six; water polo, seven; and cricket, eleven? Why are there six players in ice hockey, but eleven in its grassy equivalent?

Simple as these questions might be, they are deceptively difficult to answer. In the case of basketball, we know the game began with nine men per side because its inventor, Canadian James Naismith, was faced with a class of eighteen ruffians in a Springfield, Massachusetts, YMCA who had nothing else to do. During the harsh winter of 1891, Naismith proposed a new indoor exercise based on a then-familiar "duck on the rock" rock-throwing game. The idea was that the players would throw a soccer ball at two peach baskets nailed ten feet up at each end of the gymnasium. The janitor, who had been tasked with retrieving the balls from the baskets, tired of scaling the gym's walls and cut holes in the baskets instead (though at least one source has it that holes weren't cut in the baskets until twenty-one years later).[1] Peach baskets continued as common currency for the games over the next fifteen years, until, in 1906, metal hoops on backboards were introduced. Small indoor courts may have forced a reduction from eighteen to ten players, but precisely how and when remains vague.[2]

For other ballgames, it is quite likely that most began the way children's games still do today: by dividing whoever happens to have turned up into opposing teams. The oldest of these may well be the game of Ba', which has been played more or less continuously in Kirkwall since the mid-1600s. Kirkwall is a city on the Orkney Islands just off Scotland's northern coast. Twice a year, on Christmas and New Year's Day, Kirkwall's citizens meet at St. Magnus Cathedral to divide into two groups. The Doonies are those traditionally born close to the ocean; the Uppies, within the city's walls. Dressed in whatever seemed convenient that morning (but no attempt to coordinate), the two teams organize into a scrum around a locally produced four-pound, black-and-brown-striped ball (called the ba'). The object of the game is simple: the Doonies push the ball toward the ocean over a mile-long course, while the Uppies push in the opposite direction. If the Doonies succeed in submersing the ba' in seawater, they win. The Uppies prevail if they are able to push the ball uphill beyond a predefined city line. Because newcomers to Kirkwall tend to locate within the city walls, the Uppies outnumber the Doonies, so some 110 Doonies may fight for possession of the ba' with 200-odd Uppies in a game that has run anywhere from four minutes to nine hours.[3]

Similar historical novelties include folk soccer games where teams were made up entirely arbitrarily—married men versus bachelors or village against village—on a playing field of random lengths. The distance between two goals could be as long as several miles, as in Ashbourne, Derbyshire, where a game of soccer is still played every Shrove Tuesday (referred to today as Royal Shrovetide Football) by pitting two teams of the town's citizens against each other on a field three miles in length.[4] This game began well before Cambridge University students wrote soccer's first rule book in 1848, which was subsequently codified in 1863, nailing the issue of size once and for all. The Aussies did so for Australian football in 1858; the Canadians, for ice hockey in 1877; and the Americans, for volleyball in 1895. Presumably, smaller playing fields and smaller teams were thought to produce more exciting play (not least for the spectators), leading both field and teams to shrink considerably. But why football teams stopped at eleven members and not nine or twelve, or water polo at four and not five is not obvious, except that the majority of team sports seems to have settled for odd numbers.

Whatever the historical reasons, numbers in sports teams have solidified in a way they haven't in the workplace. Most organizations vary the size of their teams depending on the various skills they require for the task at hand, occasionally differentiating between core and peripheral team members. These teams can vary greatly in size, from project teams of four to ten in litigation to an eye-watering twenty-seven hundred scientists collaborating across thirty-four nations in the case of the $6 billion Large

Hadron Collider.[5] But what do we really know about the relation of team size to productivity? Are people likely to work
harder or less hard than they would individually when part of a
team? And what does this depend upon?

The Ringelmann Effect

One of the earliest attempts to scientifically investigate the relation between team size and productivity dates back to the 1880s,
and the French agricultural engineer Max Ringelmann
(1861–1931). A curious feature of these early experiments is that
the location of Ringelmann's original report has always been
somewhat of a mystery. Written between 1882 and 1887, it seems
to have gotten "lost" until rediscovered and promptly republished
in 1986. However, his experimental findings had by then already
become the stuff of legend.

So what exactly did he discover? In a set of simple rope-pulling
trials, he asked volunteers to pull as hard as they could on a five-
meter horizontal rope spun along a garden path.[6] Ringelmann
would diligently record their strongest pull, both individually and
collectively, during a four- to five-second period of maximum
collective exhortation. The device of choice was a simple
dynamometer, a device for measuring force. Unsurprisingly perhaps, his numbers showed a decrease in power per individual as
teams grew in size. What no one had expected was the sheer
extent of the decrease: two subjects pulled at 93 percent of their
capacity, three at 85 percent, and eight of them at only 49 percent
of what he knew they were capable of pulling as individuals. Thus,
eight people together pulled less hard than four individuals added
together. This deterioration in performance became known as the

Ringelmann effect, and he attributed it to the difficulty of coordinating. To pull together at maximum strength for several seconds requires coordination and comes, he thought, at a cost.

The challenge of making four plus four add up to eight—let alone more than eight—presents itself in sports, too. In crew rowing, for example, a double (featuring two oarsmen with two oars each) is only 4 percent faster than a single, whereas an eight (with each oarsman having a single, longer oar) is only 6 percent faster than a four (where, likewise, each is equipped with one oar). Even accounting for differences in water displacement, given larger boats, the addition of more rowers is associated with diminishing returns.

Subsequent generations of scholars picked up on Ringelmann's experiments, none more so than Alan Ingham, a kinesiologist best known for his contributions to the sociology of sports. In the early 1970s, Ingham and three colleagues at the University of Massachusetts, Amherst, decided to recreate the rope-pulling experiment based on what they'd been told about what Ringelmann had allegedly done. Tool kits in tow, they built a wooden structure consisting of six pulling stations and a rope tied between two frames. We should bear in mind that by this time no one had yet recovered the original Ringelmann report, and without the benefit of original specifications, Ingham and his friends assembled an apparatus that would minimize slippage while maintaining simplicity. The subjects were 102 students enrolled in an introductory psychology course. Each had joined on the promise of extra credit for participating. They were given the following instructions:

> This apparatus is designed to test your pulling power. You will be tested alone and in groups of various sizes. This is not a competition and no results will be given you until the

required number of pulls are completed. You will be given three commands:

(1) "Take the Strain." During this phase, you will have time to secure a grip on the rope and adjust your foot position. One foot must be placed on the number in the center of the footrest and your other foot on the baseboard;

(2) "Pull!" During this phase you are required to pull as hard as you can for a period not exceeding 6 sec. Pull along the line of the rope. Do not pull down or to the side, but attempt to remain in the required stance. (A second demonstration of the correct and incorrect methods of pulling was given by the model.)

(3) "Rest." You may return to the standing position and recover from your exertions.[7]

Like Ringelmann's original experiment, theirs too showed a sharp decline in performance. Two students pulled at 91 percent of capacity, three at 82 percent, and six at 78 percent. (Given space limitations, they were only ever able to build a wooden structure to accommodate teams of six.) Ingham and his colleagues subsequently asked some of the students to participate in a brilliant twist on the original trial: when next invited to join a fellow student in pulling the rope, they were to pretend they were pulling but not exercise any effort in the process. Ingham called on actors to help students fake the exertions and motions appropriate to someone pulling. All participating students were subsequently blindfolded. They hoped to test whether Ringelmann's relatively benign explanation of this rapid decrease as due to a lack of coordination was accurate or whether something more sinister was at work.

To their astonishment, their findings showed no marked difference from the original experiment. Teams of six students in which only three students were genuinely pulling only produced the output of three students pulling *as if* they were working in teams of six. In other words, it didn't seem to matter whether students were part of a larger team or simply thought they were part of a larger team, they pulled less hard. Thus, coordination as the original explanation for loss of effort had to give way to "social loafing": team members seemed to be reducing their effort because their individual contributions were no longer easily identifiable.

That behavior is shaped by perception and not reality was never exclusively Ingham's domain. As the British social anthropologist Kate Fox discovered, perception beats reality in alcohol consumption too, meaning that the effects of alcohol on behavior are determined by cultural rules and norms, not by the alcohol itself. Thus, experiments involving genuine alcoholic drinks as well as placebos suggest that when people think they are drinking alcohol, they behave according to their cultural beliefs about the effects of alcohol. These beliefs vary greatly with culture. Brits become more aggressive, more outspoken, and more flirtatious after sipping nothing more harmful than a placebo.[8]

Since Ingham's recreation of Ringelmann's original experiment, at least another eighty studies on social loafing have been published, based on a variety of tasks—some simple, some not— including shouting and swimming, but also complex tasks such as collectively generating ideas or rating poems for quality.[9] The latter types are useful in that *additive* tasks (like pulling a rope) in the workplace are relatively rare. It is far more likely that teams are *conjunctive* or *disjunctive,* meaning that they rely on people with different skill sets working in some coordinated fashion. The smartest person on the team typically determines collective performance in conjunctive tasks, such as solving a complex problem. By contrast, disjunctive ones are those where the weakest link determines performance; think of a team descending a glacier, for example.

Based on experiments with teams consisting of two to seven people solving a set of problems, psychologists Richard Hackman and Neil Vidmar discovered that people themselves tend to prefer teams of four or, at most, five members. They felt anything fewer than four too small to be effective, whereas teams larger than five became ineffective. The study itself, as Hackman admits, may not have been all that groundbreaking; Ivan Steiner, in 1972, had already suggested that teams peak at between four to five members. And the difficulty with studies of this type is that they do always not account for task variety. After all, some tasks require a much larger skill set than represented by four or five individuals. Nor do they account for some people being more skilled at managing large teams than others.[10] But they do remind us that small teams are generally better and, all other things being equal, that teams are more likely to optimize their performance when faced with slightly fewer members than the task at hand requires.[11]

In the late 1960s, United Airlines and the pilots union jointly commissioned a study designed to settle a dispute over whether flight crews should be made up of two or three individuals. The aircraft manufacturer Boeing had originally designed the 737 cockpit so that it could accommodate a three-person crew. United argued that two pilots were sufficient. Incidentally, this would generate significant savings in labor costs. The union disagreed. It argued that an increasingly busy airspace required three pairs of eyes and ears. The study's findings would not have surprised any of Ringelmann's disciples: three-member crews did no better than two-person crews. While they did leave the cockpit more frequently (these were the days before the terrorist attacks on September 11, 2001), which may have strengthened work relationships between pilots and flight attendants, the study found no evidence of additional safety provided by a third crew member. Three-member crews were no better at picking up potentially conflicting air traffic communicated to them by air traffic control than the two-member variety.[12]

In addition to social psychologists' experiments run in comfortable and well-resourced laboratories, others have been conducted "in the field."[13] For example, a 2005 study of software development teams by Quantitative Software Management found that assigning a team of twenty or more individuals to a project need not shorten its time but can result in more bugs in the software. Quantitative Software Management recommends teams of five or fewer instead.[14] A dozen or fewer is San Diego State University professor Stephen Robbins's best guess: any more and the team will find it difficult to interact constructively. John Katzenbach and Douglas Smith in their best-selling book on top management teams agree: real teams work far better when relatively small.[15] Management teams rely critically on the quality, capability, and attitude of each member, where more is not necessarily better. So does management consultant Kal Bishop, who found this to be particularly true of creative teams, with larger teams inclined to seek consensus rather than explore novel ideas.[16]

Social Loafing

So what to do about social loafing? Doing nothing is not really an option. If there is anything high performers find it difficult to accept, it is that mediocre performance is tolerated within their own teams. Not only will they react badly to loafers, but they will invariably turn against those allowing for inferior performance, and particularly when rewards are shared equally. A 2008 update to a 1998 McKinsey study, "War for Talent," found that nearly 60 percent of respondents would be delighted if their organization were quicker to dismiss underperformers, or move them to a less critical role.[17] It also suggested that 40 percent believe their line managers are unwilling to differentiate among top, average, and underperformers. And, whereas 71 percent thought candid feedback on performance was critical to their success, only 32 percent found that they received effective feedback. Thus, a team risks losing not its worst performers, but the very best.

The question then is how to tackle process losses? If a team cannot easily divide a project into individual tasks—meaning that everyone is accountable to everyone else for a very specific and easily identifiable segment—what might reenergize loafers instead? A renewed sense of urgency might help in that even when team members slack off, the additional effort of others will compensate for this slack. This requires that individuals have a very clear sense of where they are going, what is expected of them, and why what they do matters and to whom (none of which are straightforward in business). Alternatively, weaker members may feel disproportionately responsible for the failure of a project, something formally referred to as the Köhler effect.

Transparency can be a great deterrent too. Sports have the edge in that progress is measured on an ongoing basis, and in relatively objective ways. So, for example, coaches measure not just the speed of fast rowers on a fictional five-hundred meter fictional course (called a "split"), or on much dreaded 2 kilometer, 5 kilometer, and 6 kilometer erg tests, but can accurately model the shape and consistency of their rowing strokes in a carbon-fiber shell on the water. This is in addition to the sort of transparency that gym equipment provides, with weights or resistance settings, in full view of the rest of the crew.

But even subjective data can be transparent. In early 2007, the Cambridge University Boat Club began a controversial experiment. Each week, the coaching team would post not just objective performance results on the inside door of the gym but, right next to it, a sheet with five columns of subjective assessments by the coaching team. Next to a crewman's name in the first column, the coaches wrote (in a few words) what he did well in the second column, and what he didn't do so well in the third. The fourth and fifth columns were reserved for what he should stop doing and start doing without delay. The coaches' initiative left no real place to hide, and created a spirit of mutual accountability.

Few corporate environments allow for that sort of transparency, however, with the exception perhaps of professional service and brokerage firms, which record individual billings and trades and disseminate the information. Rumor has it that the experiment of providing weekly feedback on "good," "bad," "stop," and "start" did not in fact originate in crew rowing but with Kraft Foods.[18]

The Abilene Paradox

Large teams, in particular, are at risk of falling prey to a close relative of the Ringelmann effect: the Abilene paradox. Management expert Jerry Harvey coined the term after a discovery he made while visiting his in-laws on a blistering afternoon in the small town of Coleman, Texas. The incident, which he related in a filmed reenactment, is worth telling in some detail. As Harvey recalls, a strong, warm wind from the Panhandle was blowing hot Texas topsoil into every nook and cranny. Even so, staying indoors seemed worse than roughing it on the outside veranda over a game of dominoes.

As four o'clock came and went, Harvey's mother-in-law set the stage for a dreadful decision: what should they do for supper? Harvey's father-in-law was first to respond, "How about we go to have a meal at that roadside cafe in Abilene?" to which Harvey's wife replied with an expected, "Sounds like a good idea to me."

"How far is it to Abilene?" Harvey asked. Fifty-three miles, his father-in-law answered. When Harvey then asked whether he'd ever got the air-conditioning fixed in his Buick, the reply was a quick "nope." Looking first at his wife and then her mother, Harvey continued: "I'd like to but I don't want to go if your mother doesn't want to." She, thinking she didn't want to stay behind eating leftovers out of the refrigerator, agreed to the plan, and off they went.

Four hours, a miserable dinner, and 106 miles later, their already foul moods had reached boiling point. Harvey's mother-in-law was first to bat: "I wish we'd never gone on that trip. If only you hadn't pressured me." "Pressured you?" Harvey replied incredulously, before going on to blame his wife and father-in-law instead. His father-in-law confused everyone by saying he himself hadn't wanted to go in the first place. When asked why he suggested they go, he replied with a mere "I was just testing the waters. How did I know you'd all take me seriously?"[19]

This harmless incident in Texas's heartland gave rise to a powerful workplace paradox, suggesting that problems arise not because there is conflict but precisely the opposite: because there is none. The absence of conflict need not signify consent but, as was the case here, an environment not safe enough to voice disagreement. An outsider might notice nonverbal clues that suggest people aren't entirely happy with where they are going, through expressions of cynicism, sarcasm, or plain apathy. Telltale signs include finger-pointing, particularly in private, and members who are happier and more relaxed outside their teams. Those caught on the inside will often seem frustrated at the state of affairs; tempted to replay past discussions while imagining themselves as more assertive, smarter, or more courageous; and inclined to look for escape routes by reprioritizing other commitments, scheduling "more important" meetings to conflict with project-related discussions, or delegating, taking vacation time, or even sick leave.[20] As Peter Drucker quipped, "There is surely nothing quite so useless as doing with great efficiency what should not be done at all."[21] To economize on effort by not doing what needs doing is similarly pointless.

The Abilene Paradox in Sports

Corporate teams are no stranger to the Abilene paradox, but neither are sports teams. Despite commitment to a shared objective, sports teams can be experienced as psychologically unsafe by those on the inside, meaning they self-sensor for fear of retribution or of destroying whatever team spirit exists. One example entails the very same 2007 Cambridge crew introduced earlier. For the Boat Race, the crew decided to replace its longtime favorite coxswain with a much less experienced female coxswain. Russ Glenn already had two victories under his belt with Cambridge's reserve crew, whereas Rebecca Dowbiggin had never coxed a crew of this caliber in racing conditions. A former wrestler from Brown University in Rhode Island, Russ competed for Cambridge in boxing, while also preparing to take leadership of the Blue Boat crew. He was excellent at firing up suboptimal crews, his calls designed to ignite their competitive spirit and help them push through pain barriers. The selection process was his to lose; Rebecca's lack of experience meant she was never considered a serious contender until eleven days before the Boat Race.

After a dismal performance in a fixture (or a mock race against a top national crew over a section of the championship course), two of the Cambridge crewmen decided to call a meeting. They gathered as a group of eight plus two coaches, but without their coxswain, to clear the air. As they took turns talking, they discovered that they shared concerns about Glenn's coxing: his steering had not been up to scratch, and his aggressive calls made them nervous. With two reigning world champions, three additional internationals, and an Olympic gold medalist in the crew, they knew they were race favorites. They had been favorites the previous year and lost the Boat Race.

Regardless of their potential, they were anxious and worried about not being able to settle into a strong rhythm on the day of the race, when they would be flanking their Oxford rivals on the seven-kilometer championship course. They didn't need to be told to work harder; they needed to be told that things would be okay so long as they stuck with the plan and focused on coordinating their movements. They worried that Glenn's calls caused them to fret about their own performance and, even if pulling harder themselves, would not allow them to find the collective rhythm they were looking for. Even though most of them had had strong reservations about Glenn as coxswain for some time, no one had spoken up for fear of being the odd one out. Glenn was very likable and was "one of the lads," and speaking out against him risked not just personal isolation but embarrassing one of their own. The end result—a decision to replace Glenn with Dowbiggin with only ten days to go—was unfair to Glenn: not only had he lost his seat to a less experienced coxswain, but the newspapers were merciless. Glenn had been announced as the Blue Boat coxswain, and for the crew to change its mind this close to the race had a smack of desperation about it. It also left the crew with just over a week to get used to rowing with

Dowbiggin for a race for which they had spent six months preparing.[22] Led by Dowbiggin, the crew raced to victory on April 7, to win the 156th Oxford and Cambridge Boat Race.

The Abilene Paradox in Health Care

Harvard professor Amy Edmondson's work with hospital teams in the Boston area offers some startling insights into the consequences of the Abilene paradox for patient safety. Using a sample of eight nursing units, she examined the link between, on the one hand, the quality of leadership and the strength of interpersonal relationships in nursing teams and, on the other hand, errors in administering drugs to patients. Each team comprised forty staff, on average, a combination of full- and part-time nurses, physicians, pharmacists, and clerical and medical aids. Each team had a nurse manager. Edmondson collected survey data from the staff on various team characteristics, such as the amount of direction and coaching the nurse managers provided, relations among staff, and quality and style of leadership. Because the nurse managers generally had a great deal of latitude to manage teams as they saw fit, there was plenty of variation within the sample. Some teams were cohesive, tightly structured, and carefully managed; others less so. Edmondson also collected data on medication errors from reviews of patient charts and team members' voluntary reports. Her assumption was that better-managed teams were less likely to make mistakes in administering drugs than poorly managed teams.

A first glance at the collected data confirmed suspicions: the number of medication errors did vary substantially among the eight hospital nursing units and were highly correlated with team characteristics. To her surprise, however, the correlation was negative. Nursing units that might have been textbook examples of tightly managed, well-structured, and well-run teams were also those associated with the highest incidence of errors. Not just that, but this relationship held only for those mistakes that could have been avoided (rather than unexpected, drug-related complications over which the team couldn't have had any control). And the difference was considerable: teams who rated their leadership highly and who thought well of each other showed ten times the number of drug-administering errors.

Intrigued, Edmondson and her colleagues decided to conduct a series of follow-up interviews with the staff and also to observe them for short periods as they went about their everyday work. Doing so allowed her to get a more accurate sense of the varying social climates of the nursing units. When ranking the eight teams according to the openness of their climates, she discovered a near-perfect match between openness and medication errors, meaning that more errors meant better reporting of mistakes. Teams that felt psychologically safe were those in which nurses, clerks, pharmacists, and physicians were comfortable owning up to errors, whereas teams that felt psychologically unsafe did not report mistakes.[23] Armed with this information, anyone could be forgiven for picking the error-prone nursing unit over those ostensibly safer. Psychological safety in nursing teams had eradicated the Abilene paradox by encouraging members to own up to mistakes so as to learn from them.

Edmondson's subsequent study of sixteen cardiac surgery teams forced to implement a relatively new, minimally invasive, surgical procedure suggested that teams learn at different rates. She observed that differences in the ability of surgical teams to learn seems unrelated to variations in educational background and surgical experience. Nor are they related to the status of surgeons leading the different teams or levels of top management support for the new procedure. What mattered far more was the surgeons' ability to create a psychologically safe space for team members to admit mistakes, volunteer suggestions, and offer constructive criticism.[24]

There is compelling evidence from experimentation in social psychology to suggest that when individual subjects are assigned to teams and given varying bits of information, they are far more likely to seek common ground than to explore differences in the information provided to each.[25] Particularly in teams comprised of different areas of expertise, this natural tendency can greatly limit the team's ability to learn or excel. The willingness to engage in cognitive conflict is imperative to team performance, but only happens in environments the team members consider to be psychologically safe.

A related study in medicine looked at the difficulties medical teams had as a result of their unquestioned deference to experts. Specifically, researchers tested the willingness of well-trained nurses to surrender their decision-making responsibilities to the judgment of someone they thought was the attending physician. In the experiment, one of the researchers phoned twenty-two separate nurses' stations on various surgical, medical, pediatric, and psychiatric wards, identifying himself as a hospital physician and directing the answering nurse to give 20 milligrams of the drug Astrogen to a specific ward patient. In 95 percent of the cases, the nurse went immediately to the ward medicine cabinet, secured the ordered dosage of the drug, and headed straight for the patient's room.

The nurses followed orders despite the fact that the drug had not been cleared for hospital use, the prescribed dosage was twice the manufacturer's maximum daily dose, and the person giving the directive was someone the nurse had never met or even talked with before on the phone. The authors of the study concluded that in fully staffed medical units like the ones they examined, it is natural to assume that multiple "professional intelligences" cooperate to ensure that the best decisions are made. But in fact, under the conditions of the study, only one of those intelligences—the physician's—may be functioning.[26]

The Abilene Paradox in Corporate Boards

Professors Jim Westphal and Michael Bednar's analysis of 228 boards of directors of medium-sized U.S. companies provides compelling evidence for the Abilene paradox in the corporate world, using a much larger sample. Why is it, they asked, that boards so often fail to initiate strategic changes when faced with poor corporate performance?[27]

Prior research on executive decision making highlighted several cognitive biases associated with poor performance; for example, the tendency to overattribute poor performance to circumstances outside managerial control. Failure to change may also be due to the board's reluctance to admit that the current strategy isn't working, or even a conviction that with time, the tide will turn if the company stays the course. There is even evidence to suggest that poor performance leads executives to restrict their search for new information and, particularly, data that casts doubt on the effectiveness of their current strategy. Occasionally, this leads them to look outside for professional advice to affirm their assumptions and bolster their confidence. One reason for having outside directors is so they play devil's advocate and challenge explanations for poor corporate performance.

That this may work better in theory than practice is exactly what Westphal and Bednar found in their analysis. While outside directors may be more objective and less biased when it comes to evaluating corporate strategy, they are prone to precisely the sort of psychological bias of which the Abilene paradox is a particular case, namely, "pluralistic ignorance." Westphal and Bednar's results provide strong evidence of board members' failure to express their concerns with the status quo. What's more, directors greatly underestimate the extent to which their fellow directors share these concerns, with the predictable result that underperforming companies are more likely to persist with a doomed course of action. Popular examples of boards' failure to challenge corporate decisions include Royal Bank of Scotland's acquisition of ABN, and Lloyds' merger with Halifax.

So what can leaders do to boost the level of psychological safety within the teams they manage?[28] One approach is to follow the example of the Royal Navy by "deranking" when full and frank disclosure is required. Royal Navy chaplains achieve a similar effect by always assuming the rank of whoever they happen to be talking to. It is a protocol not shared by either the Royal Army or Royal Air Force, nor particularly evident in corporate life.

Team leaders can also reduce status differences by choosing to convene at a neutral location, rather than boardrooms or offices laden with symbols of hierarchy and power. If the usual culprits dominate the conversation, it might help to bring in an outside person with relevant expertise. Not only can this restore some parity, but more importantly, it tests the comparative robustness of viewpoints and the assumptions on which they are founded. Or team leaders might try to stimulate frank and open debate by removing themselves from a team meeting. If necessary, they could invite a third-party facilitator to structure the conversation and, where relevant, a subsequent debrief to those in charge. None of these alone may forever change the tone and transparency of conversations within the team, but some combination of them is likely to have a positive effect. It is also easier to do with smaller teams.

An interesting and entirely practicable antidote is to institutionalize a "donkey question," or a potentially silly question to which the answer should have been obvious to the questioner. The principle behind it is disarmingly simple. As one CEO put it to me: "As team leader I expect you to ask me one of these questions every day. You'll probably expect the answer to be obvious—or at least in hindsight—and the question silly. But that doesn't matter. You could be onto something very important. I don't want too many donkey questions, but you must promise me one for every day of the week." Unusual? Perhaps. Silly? A bit. Effective? Absolutely.

The Abilene paradox isn't the only, or even most common, thing to impact teams psychologically. As we will see in the next chapter, so is superstition. Yet it's not all bad news.

6

Why Superstition Can Be Good for Performance

The Old: There is no such thing as luck. Beliefs to the contrary are counterproductive.

The New: There is such a thing as luck. Even just believing there is can better performance.

The Challenge: To leave well enough alone.

In an example of narrow margins in sports and the effects of luck and mental toughness, Adrian Moorhouse, the world's number-one breaststroke swimmer for six years running, gave this account of the 1998 Seoul Olympics:

> I quickly looked either side of me to see whereabouts I was in the race, whether I could see any feet or bodies ahead of

me in the pool, and when I did I thought "okay, I'm behind here. I shouldn't be this far behind." I distinctly remember thinking that I was faced with two choices: "I can still win this" and "oh shoot, I'm not going to win this." In what seemed like minutes, but can only have been a few seconds, I made up my mind: "it's not over . . . I can still beat them."

And I remembered the 1984 Games, and how Britain expected me to take home gold, and how I was in a similar position and just didn't have the guts or belief that I could go on and more or less gave up. It's very much a mental process . . . And so here I was again, throwing in the kitchen sink and thinking I might actually do this. I knew that my weaknesses were the dive and turn, and with those now behind me also realized that my strength was the final sprint. This is what I was best in the world at. In the last twenty meters, I could out-swim anyone . . .

Looking back at the video now, the result was incredibly close. If there were 45 strokes in the race, I was trailing behind up until the 44th stroke. It wasn't until the 45th stroke that my hand reached for the wall . . . I didn't know who'd been fastest, and so I turned around and searched for the clock, trying to spot my name and number. Seeing I'd won I felt euphoric. Seeing I'd won by only a 100th of a second, I thought "that's not very good," and looked over at Károly Güttler, my Hungarian competitor, I felt sad for him having lost by the smallest measurable margin . . .

Then the euphoria returned, I did my BBC poolside interview, cried all along the way to the podium, was given my medal, and subsequently spent two hours trying to produce a urine sample. By the time I'd finally arrived back at the apartment, everyone had gone to sleep. And so I went to bed in my tracksuit, my medal around my neck and against my chest, unable to sleep.[1]

More recently, the American Michael Phelps earned his seventh gold (in the 100-meter butterfly) in Beijing by 1/100th of a second too. The Germans beat the Japanese in lady's team pursuit speed skating by 0.02 seconds at the Vancouver games in 2010. Sprints are typically decided by small margins; the margin between the fastest and tenth-fastest all-time 100-meter sprint is a mere 0.27 seconds.[2]

The Boat Race was won by one-half length (30 feet) or less on eight occasions (1856, 1867, 1877, 1891, 1949, 1952, 1980, 2003). The verdict was one length (60 feet of a margin of 0.27 percent over the 4-mile, 374-yard stretch) on less than seventeen occasions, out of 157 races. In all, 11 percent of them were won by less than a third of 1 percent of the distance, one of the closest results being that of 2003, when Cambridge lost to Oxford by one foot (or a margin of 0.005 percent).[3]

The margins in Formula One racing are notoriously small and shrinking: from 1950 to 1959, the average margin for each drivers' championship was 1 minute, 4.3 seconds; from 1960 to 1969, it was 46.7 seconds; from 1970 to 1979, 18.4 seconds; from 1980 to 1989, 23.6 seconds; from 1990 to 1999, 18 seconds; and from 2000 to 2009, a mere 9.9 seconds, on average.[4] The championship was decided by a single point on no fewer than seven occasions, in 1958, 1961, 1964, 1981, 1994, 2007, and 2008; more surprising still, Niki Lauda took the 1984 title by only half a point over McLaren teammate Alain Prost.[5]

Margins in sports can be uncomfortably narrow, meaning there is little to differentiate finalists physiologically. All have gone through pretty similar training and selection regimens. Margins in business and professional services can be just as small. The bids to provide audit services to a global giant can easily involve teams of one hundred or more professionals across the world working together to win the big prize. The selection committee deciding which firm to award the contract to can comprise fewer than five individuals who, in turn, solicit input from colleagues. To introduce objectivity into the selection process, they typically use a scoring system to assess the performance of each candidate firm in key areas such as quality of personnel, including insight, proactivity, efficiency, cost, and experience. Invariably, the margin between firms hovers within only a few points. Because of such small margins, luck and mental toughness take on disproportionate importance. A consequence of the latter is that elite sports teams invariably include a dedicated sports psychologist. Luck's consequences are more mysterious, yet no less ubiquitous: a retreat into superstition and pregame rituals.

Distasteful as it may be to fans, sports are not impervious to coincidence. Malcolm Gladwell's *Outliers* supplied a particularly revealing example of success in ice hockey related to birth date. Armed with data on Canadian pro hockey players and junior league hockey-team rosters, he points out something first noted by Roger Barnsley, a Canadian psychologist. In the mid-1980s, Barnsley discovered that most of the players in the major junior A league and those who went on to play professional hockey happen to have been born in January, February, or March. Gladwell noted:

> Barnsley . . . gathered statistics on every player in the Ontario Junior Hockey League. The story was the same. More players were born in January than in any other month, and by an overwhelming margin. The second most frequent birth month? February. The third? March. Barnsley found that there were nearly five and a half times as many Ontario Junior Hockey League players born in January as were born in November. He looked at all the all-star teams of eleven-year-olds and thirteen-year-olds—the young players selected

for elite traveling squads. Same story. He looked at the composition of the National Hockey League. Same story. The more he looked, the more Barnsley came to believe that what he was seeing was not a chance occurrence but an iron law of Canadian hockey: in *any* elite group of hockey players—the very best of the best—40 percent of the players will have been born between January and March, 30 percent between April and June, 20 percent between July and September, and 10 percent between October and December.[6]

Children born early in the calendar year are likely to be taller and more mature and better coordinated than those several months their junior. As a result, they are likely to receive more ice time, more attention from their coaches, and thus more chance to excel. Given that the cutoff date in Canadian hockey is set at January 1, ten-year-olds born in January might be playing with those who won't turn ten until eleven months later. Birth date is, of course, a chance event from the player's point of view, even if much less random for the kid's biological parents (and herein lies a lesson for parents eager to produce the next Jonathan Toews, a Chicago Blackhawks player).[7]

In similar fashion, soccer penalty shoot-outs give an unfair advantage to the team that shoots first, which, in turn, is decided by a simple coin toss. With few exceptions, those that win the toss choose to shoot first. Economists Jose Apesteguia and Ignacio Palacios-Huerta think they know why. They examined 2,820 penalty kicks from shoot-outs at major national and international competitions between 1970 and 2008. Their findings are uncompromising: the team that takes the first kick wins 60 percent of the time, meaning that the coin gives a 20 percent advantage to the team that shoots first.[8] The same is true for sport's cerebral cousin, chess: the player who draws the white piece in the first game wins about 60 percent of matches played.[9] Baseball scouts and coaches have caught on too: they use advanced statistical tools that can compute how much a player's accomplishments at bat stem from randomness as opposed to skill. The *Wall Street Journal*'s Russell Adam reported that Rick Hahn, assistant general manager of the Chicago White Sox, admits as much: "There is a fair amount of luck involved in this game . . . It's probably such a high amount that it could keep you up at night and eat away at your stomach lining if you let it."[10] Golfer Seve Ballesteros detested it: "I win on narrow courses, I win on open courses. I win when it's wet and I win when it's dry. I win when it's windy and I win when it's calm. Still they say I am lucky."[11]

Chance and Superstition in Sports Teams

The realization that sports are not impervious to chance may explain why superstition has long been a staple diet. Veering from the eccentric to the pathological, chance and superstition provide the illusion of control in imperfectly controllable, winner-take-all milieus. Examples are mostly well known: Canadian hurdler Angela Whyte never carries her podium clothes with her to the track at international competitions for fear of jinxing her performance. Lawn bowler David Mathie plays with the price tag still attached to his right shoe, whereas his colleague Erin Marie Roth carries a poker chip with her when playing internationally. Gymnast Catherine Dion always tightens her right grip before her left on the bars. Serena Williams doesn't change her socks when on a winning streak in a tennis tournament. Chicago Cubs relief pitcher Turk Wendell chewed four pieces of black licorice when pitching and brushed his teeth between each inning, while carefully avoiding baselines. The Dallas Mavericks' Jason Terry tries to sleep in a pair of uniform shorts that belong to next day's opponents, whereas Lance Armstrong puts his faith in a Texas pendant.[12] Former Oakland A's Jason Giambi wore a golden thong if he found himself in a slump at the plate, while Moises Alou, when concerned about losing his touch with the bat, was known to urinate on his hands.[13] Karate champion Lyoto Machida prefers to drink his.[14]

If this seems mildly amusing, just remember that many of us are really no more resistant to such illusions in everyday life. As Spyros Makridakis, Robin Hogarth, and Anil Gaba point out in *Dance with Chance*, 28 percent of Americans believe in astrology, 15 percent read their horoscopes every day or "quite often," while 70 percent of students claim that good-luck charms help them perform better academically. Many Chinese believe the color red will bring happiness, wealth, fame, and good luck, as does the number eight: Taiwanese will pay more for a packet containing eight rather than ten tennis balls.[15]

Italians omit the number thirteen from their national lottery; while more than 80 percent of high-rise buildings around the world lack a thirteenth floor. Likewise, airports typically omit a thirteenth gate and airplanes the thirteenth row, while hospitals and hotels have often done away with the room number thirteen.[16] People often avoid walking under a ladder, breaking a mirror, placing a hat on a bed,[17] or scheduling an important event on Friday the thirteenth. They hold their breath when passing a cemetery or knock on wood to avoid "bad luck." They throw salt over their left shoulders, and wish each other good luck.[18] Except, of course, in theaters where they "break a leg" instead, never name Shakespeare's Scottish play (*Macbeth*), never wear blue onstage unless combined with silver, never have a mirror or three lit candles on stage, and never use peacock feathers or whistle. On the other hand, they keep a light burning in an empty theater to ward off ghosts, and present the play's director with a bouquet of flowers stolen from a cemetery on closing night. Some people refuse to shave on Monday, do laundry, pay loans or bills on New Year's Day, wash their hair on Tuesday, buy oil on Saturday, clip nails at night, or sweep the floor after sunset.[19]

What may well account for the persistence of superstition in sports is the illusion of control it provides. Anthropologist Bronisław Malinowski, best known for his revealing diary of life with the Argonauts of the Western Pacific, documented superstitious behaviors among athletes as early as 1927. He noted that they are prominent wherever elements of chance might play a role, however minor, and when injuries can end otherwise promising careers.[20] Superstition, he reasoned, helps reduce performance anxiety and, in so doing, enhances focus and the chances of success.[21] The end justifies the means.

Buhrmann and Zaugg's study of 310 competitive high school basketball players found females to be more superstitious than males, and superstition to be strongly correlated with church attendance.[22] Another survey of fifty-nine varsity and intramural ice hockey players concluded that the higher the competitive level and (ironically) the more experienced, the greater the prevalence of superstition, regardless of gender.[23] A 1991 laboratory experiment at Springfield College in Massachusetts hypothesized that superstitions are most likely to develop among people who believe that they can exert some control over chance outcomes. Researchers asked thirty-seven participants to complete a survey, designed as a measure of belief in their control over chance events, then handed them a golf club and asked them to attempt fifty putts on a piece of artificial turf.

Participants were deemed superstitious when they continued to select the same color ball they had successfully putted previously. Combining the survey results with the putting behavior suggested that those participants who believed their actions controlled chance events were also the most likely to use a "lucky ball" after a successful putt.[24]

In an earlier investigation of superstition among 174 members of intercollegiate athletic teams at the University of Western Ontario during the 1971–1972 academic year, researchers Jane Gregory and Brian Petrie found superstitions were prevalent not just among individual athletes but within teams. Many of these related to equipment use, the order in which they entered the arena, or their playing position. Individuals, by contrast, relied more heavily on the use of charms and lucky numbers or, as still seen today, on crossing themselves before entering the playing field. Superstitions also seemed to vary by sport. Thus, hockey players cared about equipment, order, and player position; basketball teams, about sinking the last warm-up shot; and swimmers, about the color of their suit. Lane numbers mattered to track athletes, and a particular brand of ball to tennis players.[25]

Boston Celtic's guard Ray Allen abides by a strict pregame routine: a nap from 11:30 a.m. to 1:00 p.m., chicken and white rice for lunch at 2:30, a stretch in the gym at 3:45, a quick head shave, and then practice shots at 4:30. Pregame ritual need not be superstitious, of course: what lane an athlete is in matters in terms of who and how many are running, swimming, or rowing alongside you, the preferred lanes usually being the middle ones. Sinking that last shot may provide the necessary confidence needed to enter an uncertain game. Rituals, as opposed to superstitions, focus attention and trigger well-learned motor sequences and may help create a positive mind-set while taking the edge off what can often seem to be nerve-wracking experiences.

Superstition's Consequences

There are many reasons for the persistence of superstition. But what are its consequences? So what if Tiger Woods wears a red shirt on tournament Sundays as long as it helps him up his game? University of Cologne's Lysann Damisch and colleagues have begun to unravel the performance benefits of superstition by identifying its underlying psychological mechanisms in a series of four experiments.[26] In a test similar to the Springfield trial, they required twenty-eight university students to putt a golf ball. Pretests indicated that 80 percent of them believed in good luck, so to exploit this, they told some of the students that the ball they'd just been handed had "been lucky so far." As predicted, students who believed they had been handed an ostensibly lucky ball did significantly better than the control group. Their second experiment involved fifty-one female students engaged in a motor-dexterity exercise. Given a plastic cube with thirty-six balls, they were required to feed these balls as quickly as possible through one of thirty-six holes in a fixed slab. The difference was that some of these students were explicitly told that the umpire was keeping her fingers crossed, whereas the control group was not.[27] As in the previous experiment, activating superstition influenced performance, meaning that those who were told that someone was keeping her fingers crossed were quicker at completing the task.

To find out why superstition "works," Damisch and colleagues performed a set of experiments that involved memory tests and puzzles. In the first of these, they asked forty-one students to bring lucky charms and asked them questions about their charms before taking them away to be photographed. The researcher returned the lucky charms to some but not others before giving the students a short questionnaire and instructions for a memory task. The questionnaire asked all volunteers to rate their self-efficacy (how confident they were at being able to perform the task) and level of anxiety. The participants who had had their lucky charms returned to them performed significantly better than those who had not. But in preempting the exercise with a survey, the researchers were able to get a handle on the psychological state associated with superstition and performance.[28] Those equipped with their lucky charm had reported a higher level of self-efficacy than those without, suggesting that lucky charms "work" because they elevate self-belief.

The final experiment was designed to refine understanding of self-efficacy's role by differentiating between setting higher goals or persevering for a longer time with difficult tasks in that prior research had shown both to be related to self-efficacy. The experiment asked thirty-one newly selected students to form as many words as possible from a random list of eight letters. Those armed with lucky charms felt confident they would come up with a higher number and also spent a longer time looking for words before giving up.

Thus, whether operating in teams or as individuals, in athletics or everyday life, superstition "works." Provided, of course, a person takes none of it to heart. The belief in the powers of the item in play, rather than an educated appreciation of the brain's ability to self-deceive, provides the X factor. As Piercarlo Valdesolo writes in *Scientific American*, the "I can do this" feeling will wither away as soon as one realizes that nothing mystical will influence one's performance. The science of the mind will have stripped superstition of its powers.[29]

Superstition in Business

Given the premium placed on level-headedness in commercial life, we might expect superstition to be much less prevalent. Surprisingly, however, 9 percent of Americans avoid making significant purchases on Friday the thirteenth (resulting in an estimated $800 million to $900 million in "lost" business).[30] Investors sometimes take their cue from whether a NFL or AFL team wins the Super Bowl.[31]

Even stock market behavior is shaped by solar and lunar eclipses. Copenhagen Business School's Gabriele Lepori studied the effects of 362 eclipses visible anywhere in the world between 1928 and 2008, seen by the superstitious as a bad omen, by matching them against four American stock indexes: the Dow Jones Industrial Average, the S&P 500, the New York Stock Exchange Composite, and the Dow Jones Composite Average. By computing average daily returns for each index, and by comparing returns on days when eclipses occurred with those on days when they did not, Lepori discovered small but persistent effects. Eclipses not only correlate with lower than average U.S. stock returns, but this effect is amplified during periods of economic uncertainty. It is also augmented when eclipses have attracted disproportionate media attention. The latter are, of course, consistent with superstitious behavior among athletes: the more uncertainty and the better aware of this uncertainty, the more prevalent the irrational. Lepori's observation that eclipses are associated with trading volumes and that slumps in returns are reversed in the days following an eclipse supports the link with superstition.

Given that eclipses are perfectly predictable, such behavior would seem inconsistent with the efficient-market hypothesis or the idea that markets are efficient in reflecting publicly available information and leave little scope for arbitrage. Lepori's own calculations suggest that, assuming zero transaction costs, investors who sold shares before each eclipse between 1928 and 2008, only to buy them back shortly after, would have multiplied their principal fifty-five times (compared to thirty-seven times by merely holding onto their stocks). Shrewd investors will, of course, have caught on and recognized the arbitrage opportunity provided by superstition meaning that, here too, the mind saps superstition of its magic.[32]

During the last decade, there has been a notable proliferation of popular texts on the randomness of markets—*The Drunkard's Walk, Fooled by Randomness, The Black Swan, Dance with Chance, The Luck Factor,* and, perhaps the best-known even if slightly older, *A Random Walk Down Wall Street.* In his 1973 primer, Burton Malkiel suggested that a blindfolded monkey throwing darts at stock pages could do as well as seasoned investors. A Dutch team subsequently took up the challenge. They teamed up with a gorilla named Jacko and neatly outperformed the AEX (Amsterdam Exchange) index for ten consecutive years between 1999 and 2009.[33]

But chance is not confined to financial markets. For instance, such medicinal discoveries as aspirin, the contraceptive pill, penicillin, laughing gas, vitamin K, amphetamine, antihistamines, quinine, insulin, nitroglycerin, and smallpox vaccine were all discovered serendipitously. In fact, one in ten scientific papers acknowledge chance as having contributed to their breakthrough innovations.[34] Outside of medicine, popular examples of coincidence include Scotchgard, Teflon, Velcro, nylon, Post-it Notes, Kodak's Weekender camera, the technology behind the Hewlett-Packard inkjet printer (based on a coffee percolator at work), electromagnetism, photography, dynamite, the phonograph, X-rays, radioactivity, Ivory Soap, and Coca-Cola (patented, in 1886, as "Pemberton's French Wine Coca" for medicinal purposes, as a nerve and tonic stimulant, and a possible cure for headaches).[35]

It is, of course, important not to overrate luck's ability to account for performance variations in sports or markets. Yet we would be equally foolish to exclude it altogether. And it is precisely this awareness that may explain the persistence of irrational behavior among athletes and traders, if Damisch and colleagues are to be believed, which need not be a bad thing. For to the extent that superstition elevates levels of self-efficacy, teams could do worse than tolerate superstitious beliefs.

From Superstition to Mental Toughness

Aside from the benefits of enhanced self-belief through superstition, a far more tangible differentiator between elite and merely good performance is mental toughness. Sports psychologist Graham Jones and Adrian Moorhouse provide some insightful examples of what mental toughness is, and isn't. They quote former English soccer captain David Beckham describing his state of mind just prior to his match-winning penalty kick against Argentina in the 2002 World Cup: "It all went quiet. Everything was swirling around me, every nerve standing on edge. What's going on here? I can't breathe . . . I remember forcing in two big gulps of air to try and steady myself and take control . . . I was far too nervous to try to be clever. Not nervous for myself any longer. This was all about the team I was captain of. I've never felt such pressure before. I ran forward. And I kicked the ball goalwards as hard as I could."[36]

Moorhouse too recognized the importance of resoluteness in elite swimming:

> Mental toughness in swimming is absolutely crucial . . . There were a number of examples of swimmers who were very

talented but couldn't quite cope with the pressures of competing. One particular swimmer I knew would train extremely hard, but seemed to throw it away at the big events. After months of training twice a day—starting at 5am—in the last week of competition I would see him doing things out of the ordinary, like late nights, drinking, smoking . . . There was also a Russian swimmer, and competitor of mine, who I raced frequently between 1985 and 1992, who would always get the Bronze or Silver behind me. Now I don't know whether he started off believing he could beat me, but I certainly remember the time when he stopped—at the European Championships in 1989. After winning the Olympics in 1988 I broke my wrist and didn't swim for a long time—over four months. I think he thought I had quit, as I didn't race him for most of 1989. So when I turned up at the European Championships in Bonn I remember seeing him looking more confident than he had ever looked before, but surprised to see me. Then in the heats I broke the World Record and he collapsed . . . and I saw the look on his face, and it was the collapse of his mental toughness . . .[37]

In swimming the one occasion when your belief is most tested is in that "ready room" half an hour before you go out to race. You sit with your fellow finalists preparing for the upcoming battle. Most of the time I kept to myself but occasionally would look around to see how my rivals were faring . . . When our eyes met, I could see the fear, and indeed the dismantling of their own belief. I imagined them looking at me and reflecting on my successes in a resigned way, rather than building on their own as a suit of armor. They were already beaten . . .[38] In the end it simply boils down to these facts: when I thought I was going to win, I usually did; when I thought I was going to lose, I always did.[39]

Moorhouse goes straight for the jugular: to prepare for defeat is to have lost before you've even begun. It is something David Hemery knows well too. Having set a new world record in the 400-meter hurdles at the 1968 Olympics, he only managed a third place in Munich four years later, behind Uganda's John Akii-Bua and the American Ralph Mann, despite a steep increase in the intensity of his training program and with many more miles under his belt than in 1968. The difference that time, as he now acknowledges, was that his preparation had been driven by his fear of losing. Even as he walked out of the ready room onto the track for the Olympic final, Hemery was nowhere near as pumped up as four years earlier. This frightened him. He commented, "I made my hands into fists, pushing my fingernails into my hand, telling myself 'Wake up, David! This is it . . . this is the Olympic final.'"[40] Though he had run this distance countless of times in training, he front-loaded his race and ran out of steam in the last hundred. In preparation he had imagined himself being outrun on the track—and so he was.

Similarly, former New Zealand international rower Duncan Holland refers to the "caught in the headlights" effect to describe the phenomenon of a relatively junior rowing crew unable to leverage their advantage when ahead in a race. Surprised to find themselves leading the pack, they would fail to build on their speed and win the race, simply because they were never prepared to beat more experienced crews.

This lack of self-belief is hardly unique to elite athletes. Occasionally referred to as the "impostor syndrome," it denotes the inability of individuals to internalize their accomplishments.[41] Perhaps surprisingly, given the popular image of corporate chieftains as dispassionate and rational, close-up studies of senior executives reveal that those at the very top believe they fooled those around them into thinking they are smart and competent when they may be neither. Many of them are convinced they do not merit the dizzying heights they have scaled and worry that, one fine day, they will be found to be less able than people always held them to be. They often describe their experience as "feeling like a fraud," not realizing that those around them may be equally mystified by their own success. Self-doubt and negative feedback weigh heavily on their minds, and praise barely registers. Every failure is confirmation of their innate lack of ability, whereas every success is an accident. Every positive is a false positive.[42] Ironically, they frequently explain their own success (though not that of others) is due to having been in the right place at the right time.

The original 1978 study that helped identify the imposter's syndrome applied specifically to successful women. Since then, it has been shown to apply to their male counterparts, too, particularly entrepreneurs, actors, and academics. And its consequences can be costly: athletes fail to reach their true potential by holding back when facing the possibility of success—they freeze in the headlights—or will worry more about not losing than winning. In the workplace, employees fail to put themselves forward for promotion opportunities, they are less likely to take risks, or they will procrastinate. After all, every new project may unwind their carefully orchestrated charade of competence.[43] Of course, we cannot help but wonder whether it is precisely this worry about being unmasked that drives athletes and executives alike to superior performance. Perhaps this is what Australian rugby international John Eales meant when, in team selection, he would focus on those single most distinguishing features of high performers: restlessness and discontent. It is what his former coaches saw in him, and what he took to be a prime criterion for his team selection. And in some ways, this may explain the syndrome's persistence, too. After all, what might a person risk losing when eradicating all self-doubt? What price is too high a price to pay for contentment?

In sum then, the world teams inhabit is one of small margins. These small margins force them to focus not just on the rigors of objective performance data but to cling to relatively tenuous beliefs and superstition. In the next chapter, we return to the use of data, specifically when it comes to team member selection.

7

Why So Much Depends on So Little That Is Quantifiable

The Old:	Out with intuition. In with sabermetrics.
The New:	Return to intuition. It may well be our only sustainable source of advantage.
The Challenge:	How to use numbers to ask the right questions.

Michael Lewis's best-selling *Moneyball* has all the hallmarks of a good story: colorful characters, cutting-edge analytical data, the excitement of novelty, and the thrill of competitive sports. That said, it isn't so much a book about baseball—though it is that— as it is about the business of arbitrage or the process of identify- ing inefficiencies in the market for players. Thus, Lewis makes much of the Oakland A's ability to identify and then buy under-valued players by developing them and then selling them as they become more valuable. Doing so allows the A's to pocket a generous margin that can be reinvested in player development. It is this ability to spot inefficiencies by using basic statistical tools that has allowed the A's to punch well above its weight: in the American League West in 2002, it ranked highest with the least money. And the Oakland A's are not alone in leveraging scarce resources: the New England Patriots became only the second team to win three Super Bowls in four years under coach Bill Belichick, even as their payroll is ranked twenty-fourth in the football league.

But *Moneyball* is also about the rift between the "old" and "new" schools of team-member selection and about how hard it is for reason and analysis to get a foothold in a world powered by intuition, emotion, and tradition.[1] Here, Lewis characterizes the old-school approach to selection: "You found a big league ballplayer by driving 60,000 miles, staying in a hundred execrable motels, and eating God knows how many meals at Denny's all so you could watch 200 high school and college baseball games inside of four months, 199 of which were completely meaningless to you."[2]

The time-honored system was flawed. The A's general manager, Billy Beane, knew this. It was the system that had picked him. Two decades before Lewis's excursion into the A's inner circle, Beane had been one of the most coveted drafts in Major League Baseball. *Pittsburgh Post-Gazette's* Brian O'Neill leaves little to the imagination: "When Billy Beane was in high school, every baseball scout in America yearned for him. Fast, strong and handsome, he seemed to have been custom-made for the diamond. Beane scooped up his bonus money, started playing the game for pay and, boy, did he stink."[3]

Using Numbers in Team Sports

The new-school approach took its cue from a self-published pamphlet by George William James in 1977: *The Bill James Baseball Abstract.* James skillfully used the vast amount of data available on past games to make predictions about the value-added of individual ballplayers, a technique he referred to as *sabermetrics.*[4] When comparing statistics for two baseball legends, Johnny "the Needle" Pesky, in 1942, and Dick "Dr. Strangeglove" Stuart, in 1960, James argued that sabermetrics provided an objective means of figuring out who was, in fact, the more effective ballplayer. Pesky ran a high batting average but had relatively few home runs to his name. Stuart hit a high number of home runs but, by contrast, had a modest batting average. To find out who was more valuable, James developed a formula based on the assumption that the value of a player is determined by his ability to create runs for his team:

$$\text{Predicted number of runs} \quad = \quad \frac{(\text{Hits} + \text{Walks}) \times (\text{Total Bases})}{(\text{At bats} + \text{Walks})}$$

In his formula, hits and walks reflect the ability of a team to get runners on base, whereas total bases reflect its ability to move runners already on base. Thus, in 1942, Johnny Pesky had 620 at bats, 205 hits, 42 walks, and 258 total bases, meaning he generated 96 runs for his team. Dick Stuart in 1960 had 532 at bats with 160 hits, 34 walks, and 309 total bases for 106 runs created. In 1960, Dick Stuart generated ten more runs for his team than did Johnny Pesky in 1942, meaning that he was the more valuable ballplayer.[5] Wrote Alan Schwartz in the *New York Times*: "The cardinal precept of statisticians, at least within the foul lines of baseball, is that one must not accept any declaration on simple faith. Never let anything breathe the air of blithe acceptance when it can be smothered in ream upon ream of data-driven analysis."[6]

Bowling Green State professor Jim Albert has successfully used the Pesky and Stuart example to persuade his undergraduate mathematics students of the merits of statistics and probability theory. His alternative textbook, *Teaching Statistics Using Baseball*, was written precisely because he could see students tuning in to sports with the same passion that conventional data sources like crime or health care left them stone cold. Relying on James's analysis of baseball, he ventured into such issues as the relationship between runs scored and number of wins, pitching ability, and short spurts of superior performance. When, as James did, he compared the number of runs produced and allowed, and the number of wins and losses during a season for a large number of recent major league teams, he discovered that the ratio of a team's wins to losses is approximately equivalent to the square of the ratio of runs scored to the runs allowed. As a result, a manager can use this relationship to measure a batter's performance in terms of the number of wins that the player creates for his team.

Similar approaches apply to pitching performance. Albert, for example, cites a formula developed by John Thorn and Peter Palmer in *Total Baseball* that compares the average runs allowed per inning for all teams in the league with the number of innings pitched by a particular pitcher (resulting in a figure that represents the number of runs a pitcher would allow if he were average).[7] By subtracting the actual number of runs allowed, we can easily see whether a particular pitcher is below or above average—a measure that, Thorn and Palmer argue, is more useful than the traditional earned run average (ERA) statistic.

That ERA numbers remain useful is clear from the sabermetrics of sports economist J. C. Bradbury. In *The Baseball Economist,* Bradbury argues that the performance of pitchers varies with the pitching coach.[8] So, for example, when running the numbers for pitchers playing for Leo Mazzone—formerly with the Atlanta Braves and often described as one of the best pitching coaches in recent history—it is evident that pitchers performed better under him than others. Starters Jaret Wright and John Burkett, for example, or relievers Mike Remlinger and Chris Hammond, as well as Denny Neagle, Greg Maddux, and Russ Ortiz had their best performances under Mazzone. In his analysis, Bradbury accounted for noncoaching-related factors that might influence performance, including age, league, defense, and ballparks (some ballparks are bigger and easier to pitch in than others).[9] Yet even when controlling for these, he discovered that the Mazzone effect lowered pitchers' ERA by 0.62, essentially turning a mediocre pitcher with a 4.10 ERA into a quite valuable one at 3.48.[10]

Sabermetrics have also been used to dispel popular myths, such as a ballplayer having "hot hands." As Albert points out, these periods of hot and cold hitting may simply reflect the same natural variability observed in the repeated tossing of a coin. Indiana University's Chris Albright, having scoured a bulk of baseball hitting data, concluded that there is little statistical evidence for hot hands, meaning that the flipping of a coin is as good a predictor as is data from past games.[11]

The hot-hands delusion applies both to teams and to individuals. As University of Chicago professor Toby Moskowitz and *Sports Illustrated* writer Jon Wertheim explain in *Scorecasting,* a study of the Philadelphia 76ers during the 1980–1981 season by three academics, two from Cornell and one from Stanford, found no evidence whatsoever of successful field goals or free throws predicting success the next time around. However well a player fared on one attempt had no bearing on his next. When they looked at Cornell's basketball teams, they again found no evidence of hot hands. As Moskowitz and Wertheim point out, what's interesting is that players themselves believed in the hot-hands effect, as did their fans. Eighty-four percent of fans surveyed believed that "it is important to pass the ball to someone who has just made several shots in a row."[12]

John Huizinga and Sandy Weil looked at all NBA basketball games between 2002 and 2008. Again, they found no evidence of hot or cold hands. However, they did notice something interesting: players who successfully made a shot were more likely to make their next attempt a harder one. And they are 10 percent more likely to take their team's next shot. Every team member playing this way could end up costing a team 4.5 wins per season.[13] Moskowitz and Wertheim's very own study of thirty-five hundred NBA games between 2005 and 2009 went even further in suggesting that not only is there no evidence of a momentum in basketball but there is a reversal in fortunes following a winning streak: "If a team scores six or more unanswered points in the previous minute, it will on average be outscored by its opponent (by 0.31 points) over the next minute."[14] Thus, while perhaps cold and detached in comparison to old-fashioned intuition, sabermetrics has much going for it: historically, its predictions have come close to the actual records of most baseball and basketball teams.

Moneyball clearly struck a chord with baseball enthusiasts and corporate audiences alike. The term itself entered the lexicon of baseball: teams that appear to value sabermetrics are often said to be playing "moneyball." Yet despite its reception, the book—and Beane's approach to selection—is not without critics. The A's success, some argue, may have largely been due to three star pitchers: Tim Hudson, Barry Zito, and Mark Mulder. Hudson had already been drafted before Beane became general manager.

Zito and Mulder were arguably first-round picks out of top college programs that any general manager would have taken. And Beane may have got it wrong with at least five players; he was happy when other clubs drafted them, yet they went on to become star players.[15]

Nor are the Oakland A's the only small-market team to win with a modest payroll. The Seattle Mariners spent more than the A's but a lot less than the New York Yankees. The Anaheim Angels won the World Series in 2002 with a midlevel payroll. Another baseball team, the Tampa Bay Rays, won an American League pennant using similar methods, under the leadership of two former Goldman Sachs partners and a former Bear Stearns analyst. The Rays' phenomenal success is chronicled in Jonah Keri's *The Extra 2%.*

What is also noticeable about the way Beane selects players is the absence of any evidence on how individual players influence the performance of those around them. Given that baseball is the ultimate team sport, one might reasonably expect that the performance of individual players is at least partly a consequence of those they play with. So, for example, a particular pitcher-catcher combination may work better than would any arbitrary selection.

In tennis, some players appear better off as doubles partners than single players. Consider, for example, Leander Paes and Mahesh Bhupathi. With very few notable individual accomplishments, together they have won Wimbledon, the Australian Open, the U.S. Open twice, and the French Open three times. Are these sorts of synergies something that intuition is better at gauging than numbers are? How different are sports from workplace teams when we use stats to arrive at the optimal configuration of individual players?

Then there are players like basketball's Shane Battier who add significant value to their team even if their own numbers barely register. As Michael Lewis writes in an article about basketball, Battier doesn't score many points, snag many rebounds, block many shots, steal many balls, or dish out many assists. Yet when he is on the court, his teammates get better and his opponents worse.[16] The difficulty is that little of Battier's impact is measurable in any traditional sense (except via the "plus-minus" route). He takes few shots, preferring instead to pass the ball to his teammates, and commits few turnovers. He has a knack for reducing the shooting percentages of the NBA's most prolific scorers while improving the defensive efficiency of his own team.[17] Yet little of this shows up in the usual stats, making them a poor predictor of Battier's influence on the game.

Finally, the problem with a purely statistical approach to selection is glaring: as opposed to the old scouting methods that relied on the beauty of a swing or the strength of a player's arm, the approach is far too easily replicated, meaning that the success of Lewis's book may well have been to the A's disadvantage.

Other sports increasingly use statistical analysis, too. In November 2010, the Rugby Football Union began experimenting with a device that allowed coaches to keep tabs on the comparative well-being of players during a game. The device, the size of a small wristwatch and worn in an inside pocket of a neoprene undershirt, has a heart-rate monitor and a global positioning system (GPS). Information on how far players have run and at what speeds and how tired they are is relayed in real-time to the staff's handheld devices. This allows them to make decisions on replacing players who show a dip in performance or are tired. In contrast to old-school approaches, the staff makes decisions that are based on real-time, hard data, rather than perception, and should be easy to justify. As John Flanker, a former rugby captain and coach, explained: "The GPS/heart monitor allows us to monitor players and the coaches to make correct substitutional decisions. Our strength and conditioning people calculate individual profiles for all players so we know how a player can run a certain distance at a certain speed. Then we shall know when they are at the point of no return, a fatigue level that tells us he's spent."[18] AC Milan, one of Europe's finest soccer teams, likewise heavily relies on predictive models generated by its very own Milan Lab research center.[19]

Beane's obsession with numbers has also made inroads into English soccer, most recently via John W. Henry's purchase of the Liverpool Football Club.[20] Henry, along with his partner Tom Werner, had in fact tried to hire Beane as general manager upon taking the reins of the Boston Red Sox in 2002. Failing at that, he hired Bill James as a consultant instead. When taking over the debt-ridden Liverpool team, Henry likewise expressed an eagerness to involve himself in the club's strategic direction.[21] No sooner was Liverpool's commitment to sabermetrics made public, then it made headlines with a £35 million acquisition of Newcastle's Andy Carroll. Paradoxically, given Carroll's few Premier League appearances, only forty-one, the purchase price was considered well in excess of what Beane's methods would warrant as justifiable.[22] Then again, with the loss of a key player, cash to burn, and only a few hours remaining in the midseason transfer window, Liverpool's ideology may have given way to exigency.

Using Numbers in Business

Thomas Davenport and Jeanne Harris's best-selling *Competing on Analytics* is probably the most well-known attempt at illustrating how statistical analysis has come to the fore in corporate life.[23] Whereas early traces of statistical analysis appeared in Frederick Winslow Taylor's attempt to codify and standardize the practice of management, it only really went mainstream with the advent of personal computers.[24] Although companies had used room-size mainframe computers as decision support systems since the 1960s, the spread of cheap computing power and sophisticated statistical software in the 1970s and 1980s permitted organizations to chew through vast reams of data, churning them into explanatory and predictive models to support decision making. Analysis became even easier with the widespread use of the Internet and increased storage capacity. Organizations now capture and integrate "clickstream" records generated by Web sites with demographic and behavioral data on data storage devices the size of which would once have been unimaginable.[25]

Customer relationship management (CRM) and supply chain management software has allowed organizations to seamlessly integrate demand and supply chains, to minimize inventories, and to adjust their pricing by distribution channel.[26] And the use of the software is widespread: corporations as varied as Anheuser-Busch and Mars (consumer products), CEMEX and John Deere (industrial products), AstraZeneca and Vertex (pharmaceuticals), FedEx and UPS (logistics), Google and Netflix (e-commerce), and Amazon and Walmart (retail) all rely heavily on sophisticated number crunching to squeeze the last bit of performance from their systems. What helps, of course, is the availability of data on everything from purchasing behavior to credit ratings and, thanks to Facebook and LinkedIn, to professional and friendship networks.

Companies can use this data creatively to predict behavior in all sorts of ways. For example, they can use credit scores to price insurance premiums and even make employment decisions. As University of Missouri's Mark Oleson explains, "it is uncommon to counsel individuals with financial problems who don't have other kinds of problems. You're more likely to miss days at work, be less productive on the job, as well as have marriage and other relationship problems if you are struggling financially. It makes sense that if you have a low credit score that you are more likely to have problems in other areas of life. Employers looking to screen a large number of applicants could easily see a credit score as an effective way to narrow the field."[27]

So where did this use of data start in earnest? One likely place is Capital One, originally a division of Signet Bank, created by two financial service consultants in 1988. Unable to interest national retail banks in exploiting stats to target particularly profitable groups of credit customers, Richard Fairbank and Nigel Morris were given a shot by the Virginia-based Signet Bank. The pair spent two years trawling through Signet's customer data and discovered that the bank's most lucrative markets were those customers who borrowed large sums of money on their credit cards and paid off the balance in small increments. Even if this seems obvious today, at the time, the bank treated these customers much the same as those charging small purchases to their cards and paying their balance in full each month. The opportunity presented itself: why not introduce balance transfers that allow customers to consolidate debts on a single Capital One card? Customers with no, or poor, credit ratings (or subprime customers) thus became a prime source of revenues, not least through late-payment and overlimit fees. Managing the data required the construction of one of the largest databases in the world.[28]

Using Numbers in Medicine

Medicine too has been affected by sabermetrics. The American psychologist Paul Everett Meehl caused a hullabaloo in the 1950s when suggesting that clinicians would be best off using formulas to make decisions about prognosis and treatment of mentally ill patients.[29] Many judgments, he argued, are best made statistically, not intuitively.[30] His claim was bolstered by his review of twenty studies comparing decisions based on numbers and intuition, finding that only once did the latter outperform the former. In a foreword to a new edition of his landmark epistle, published in the mid-1990s, he increased this tally to 136 studies. Of these, no more than 5 percent found intuition to be more accurate than statistics in making predictions about patients.[31] One study in particular provided strong evidence that a combination of five Minnesota Multiphasic Personality Inventory scales outperformed the best intuitive judgment from among thirteen clinicians.[32] As Meehl dryly mused, "when you check out at a supermarket, you don't eyeball the heap of purchases and say to the clerk, 'Well it looks to me as if it's about $17.00 worth; what do you think?' The clerk adds it up."[33]

As with sports teams, however, the use of sophisticated statistical tools is easily replicated. Consequently, it is unlikely to be a sustainable source of competitive advantage. As Davenport and Harris admit, some of the pioneers in mining data for the purposes of yield management have not fared well. American Airlines and United Airlines, for example, long used statistical analysis to drive the pricing of seats, route optimization, and crew scheduling, yet neither were able to turn it into a sustainable differentiator. Why not? One of the principal reasons, they think, is that analytics are of little use if they support an obsolete business model. Relative newcomers such as Southwest and JetBlue (in the United States) and Ryanair and EasyJet (in Europe) are able to compete on a lower-cost basis by flying only one type of aircraft. Doing so saves on parts and crew training. And a point-to-point, rather than hub-and-spoke, route system generates further efficiencies.

The low-cost formula is nearly impossible for existing airlines to replicate, as British Airways discovered with its subsidiary, Go. Besides, the loyalty programs that American and United pioneered are unlikely to generate genuine loyalty if not matched by a differentiated standard of customer service. Low-cost carriers like Southwest have been recipients of customer service awards, as larger carriers floundered. And as in baseball, airlines can easily replicate yield management techniques; discount carriers alike rely on sophisticated seat-pricing and route-scheduling techniques to optimize profit margins. Access to data is easy and numerically proficient college graduates are plentiful.

Graduate recruitment, in fact, is one area where stats have become common currency. With easy access to SAT, GMAT, GRE, and MBTI scores, the challenge is to numerically capture such intangibles as a person's temperament, the ability to push through pain, a willingness to learn, and the ability to work with others in a team. Such subjective variables are, however, at best only partly reflected in objective performance data. Thus, scouts and coaches are once again heading back to roadside motels, crammed with new ideas for capturing soft, character-based data. As Indianapolis Colts President Bill Polian explains, scouts are likely to talk not just with a prospect's college and high school coaches but will interview his junior high school coach as well. And they will subject potential recruits to a battery of psychometric tests, measuring not just brute intelligence but a willingness to learn.[34] Heavy-handed perhaps, even intrusive but, as MIT's Michael Schrage points out, what character traits should firms overlook when preparing to offer a seven- or eight-figure compensation package?[35] That you cannot measure something doesn't mean it isn't important.

How to Identify Talent in Teams

As Jim Collins points out in his best-selling *Good to Great,* the very best companies select new talent based not on formulas but on the value of character attributes—such things as commitment, work ethic, and the capacity to grow—or the sort of stuff that is extraordinarily difficult to measure in any conventional way. This observation lies at the crux of a recent corrective for the predominance of statistics in talent scouting.

While unintentional, author George Anders provides powerful medicine for those preoccupied with numbers in team selection. In *The Rare Find,* he supplies plentiful examples of talent scouting in such varied fields as baseball, the FBI, the elite Special Forces, the Teach For America program, surgery, computer science, auditing, and university administration. What's more, Anders claims that the talent-hunting principles that characterize the best players in each of these fields are universal. Each prioritizes character over experience.

Some of his more interesting examples include the value that Special Forces selectors place on such mundane things as a soldier's demeanor and physical appearance when exhausted, hungry, rain-drenched, cold, and with no immediate prospect of reprieve. Is the soldier still constructive or has he become cynical? Are the straps of his rucksack tidy or all over the place? What happens when soldiers go out on a nighttime navigation test, supplied with only a five-color map, a compass, and a protractor, and are able but forbidden to take shortcuts by resorting to a paved road? Given the harsh and unforgiving terrain, as candidates fall behind schedule, the paved alternatives are tempting. What most of these soldiers won't realize is that a sergeant armed with night-vision goggles is watching the road to spot those resorting to the easy option. Who will continue to do the right thing even if no one is watching? As one officer tells Anders: "Men who make it into the Green Berets are likely to end up on overseas deployments with faint supervision and a lot of open-ended responsibility. They may be given $50,000 to buy months of supplies in whatever local markets they can find. There will be little formal accounting of how that money is spent."[36]

FBI selection can be similarly resourceful. After a ten-hour hike across rugged terrain, candidates are told to prepare testimony for a simulated court case. They have no food during the hike, and there is none inside the conference room. Midway through the exercise, someone walks in with a plate of delicious smelling fried chicken. However, as Anders explains, the game is rigged: there are only four pieces of chicken and six candidates. Who will eat at the expense of those equally hungry, and who will resist the temptation? When people might have to spend weeks together living in cramped conditions, it is important to know how they will react under difficult circumstances.[37]

Anders provides various other examples too. Basketball coaches focus on how college players respond to team huddles, coaches' instructions or criticisms, or to their own mistakes. Facebook recruits some of its most savvy and highest-performing candidates using puzzles posted on its Web site, such as how to write a program that can accurately identify intoxicated users who can no longer type properly. In another puzzle, Facebook's Puzzle Master Jonathan Hsu embedded his e-mail address in an obscure computer language (called Piet, after the Dutch artist Piet Mondrian), which converted the address into an abstraction of the letter f (the obscurity was such that only forty-two people caught on in two-and-a-half years . . . which is great if you only need to recruit forty-two people). David Evans, founder of the computer science department at the University of Utah, recruited restless young programmers who might not have had a hope in hell of a job anywhere else, given their unusual résumés. Yet it was this very group that helped create Pixar, Netscape, and the early Apple Macintosh computers.[38]

So it seems we face a conundrum. On the one hand, intuition outperforms judgments based on considerably more data and more time for reflection.[39] On the other, intuition is fallible: we adopt behaviors that work even if the reason we think they work isn't close to being accurate. Moreover, as humans, we suffer a plethora of cognitive biases: the tendency to place more weight on recent events, anthropomorphism, illusory correlation, bounded rationality, and information overload. In the final analysis, the question is, when should we run with the numbers and when with the gut? Intuition may well end up drawing the short end of the stick.

Unless, of course, the two factors are not as mutually exclusive as is often assumed. For example, studies of expert pathologists found that accuracy increases when they combine intuitive with statistical assessments in predicting cancer survival rates.[40] In the managerial sphere, Robert Blattberg and Stephen Hoch's extensive review of five different forecasting scenarios found that an equally weighted combination of intuition and analysis outperformed either of these decision modes in isolation.[41] Dixon's Nick Wilkinson, while fond of number crunching himself, thinks both are equally effective. He tells of a senior colleague who, ignoring the numbers Wilkinson was fond of using, would spend his Saturdays in a corner of one of his stores instead. He would take his cues from watching customers interact with the products and salespeople. Numbers meant little to him. Observing the people in his target market going about their everyday business did. In terms of performance, neither did better than the other.

In team sports, too, some of the world's best coaches rely on the combination of numbers and guts in managing teams. After all, analysis is not synthesis, and even the most comprehensive formulas risk excluding stuff that will lie forever beyond the grasp of actuaries: the sparkle in a young athlete's eyes, fatigue or low morale on the face of another, resentment among team members, fear, passion, apathy, worry. While consequential, there are yet no formulas to meaningfully capture the mood in a locker room at halftime or the anxiety of a group of MBA students after an all-nighter preparing for a case presentation the next morning. And perhaps we don't need formulas to do this. All we need is to be able to ask the right questions, and good data helps in knowing what questions to ask when.

Conclusion

What Can We Really Learn About Teams from Sports?

So the individuals have it. There is an *I* in teams. But teams have it too. Teams are driven to high performance, but only by virtue of the individuals within them. This conclusion is much less obvious than it sounds, for team leaders need to understand the idiosyncrasies, ambitions, and anxieties of those in their charge. Only by knowing and then playing to these will a team ever fulfill its potential. People, after all, do what they do for their own reasons, not yours or anyone else's for that matter. Occasionally, these reasons include the organization but there is no reason why they must. Often people will take into account the welfare of others. Most frequently, however, their reasons revolve around themselves. To that extent, elite sports and business are perhaps the purest of Darwin's worlds in that only the fit survive. This

147

makes them particularly interesting to those relegated to arm-chair philosophizing.

This book is not a guide to creating a fairer or happier world. This was never the intention. Instead, I tried to provide a realistic assessment of teams of high performers that, occasionally, also turn out to be high-performing teams. The available evidence, discussed in the book, suggests that to turn teams of high performers into high-performing teams, inequality may be useful, that conflict happens even as intentions are perfectly aligned, that likability can triumph over technical competence (suggesting that "high performance" in a team context must include some measure of social and emotional intelligence), and that too much harmony can actually hurt team performance. In that sense, this book is faithful to the lived experience of those who inhabit high performance teams. It takes people for what they are, not for what they might be. It assumes that people are in principle self-interested, and that no matter how genuine the effort of senior management, a rallying cry around the firm's mission will only have limited traction.

There are, of course, exceptions. Teams of military surgeons—such as those I had the privilege of studying firsthand in Afghanistan's Helmand province, for example, were able to rally together quickly when faced with a major casualty. As soon as a severely injured soldier or local national arrived they formed a protective shell around him, giving him the best possible care while remaining thoroughly humane in their interactions. In that sense, the key to effective teamwork is disarmingly straightforward: provided they are capable, give people something to care about more than themselves. The problem is that while you can do so occasionally, you cannot do it persistently. Not even in war. Let alone sports or business.

When these surgeons have little or nothing to do workwise, they turn on each other instead. Unable to sit still, they begin to interfere in each other's affairs, to criticize other's treatments, or to compete for work. Even when work is plentiful, they may compete for the most interesting jobs. The life-and-death scenarios they face should infuse their profession with meaning, yet they are sufficiently reflective to appreciate the futility of much of what they do. They chose to be soldiers and yet often are privately critical of the war effort. They experience periods of great intensity following long periods of boredom, yet cannot relax or do something productive. Boredom in this case is never a respite from anxiety, but the experience of anxiety without the means of alleviating it by being productive. That, alas, is a subject for another book.

In summary then, humans organized in teams are refreshingly different from automata. Their shared humanity is a cacophony of qualities: genius, suspicion, frailty, fallibility, altruism, self-centeredness, superstition, pride, and anxiety. These sorts of attributes account for process losses, disagreements, and, ultimately, relational conflicts. They explain why some combinations of people work better than others, and when it can make sense to trade likability for competence. They explain why perfectly functional teams can occasionally feel dysfunctional to those on the inside. The qualities that make team members attractive can make them difficult too, and problems arise even if conflict is far from anyone's mind.

But a team's humanity also holds the key to its effectiveness in that having recognized the vulnerability of others we may allow ourselves to be vulnerable in turn, able to connect by means of a shared humanity. They, like we do too, struggle with what Stanford University's James March refers to as the great conflicts of life: a predilection toward equality and modesty but also an urge to power and self-assertion; a commitment to rationality and the pursuit of self-interest but also a conception of duties and the pursuit of justice; a claim of human significance but so too an awareness of human absurdity and mortality.[1] It is here that we come to understand our belligerence, competitiveness, and asperity as proportionate to the insecurities they help us hide.

By implication, team leaders may choose to increase their reliance on sophisticated technological gadgets to up performance but will only ever be effective when they use these tools to unlock that basic, shared humanity. And, then, not by dispensing solutions, but by knowing what questions to ask and when.

One of my favorite sportswriters and novelists and an accomplished U.S. junior tennis player, the late David Foster Wallace, said this: "It may well be that we spectators, who are not divinely gifted as athletes, are the only ones able truly to see, articulate, and animate the experience of the gift we are denied. And that those who receive and act out the gift of athletic genius must, perforce, be blind and dumb about it—and not because blindness and dumbness are the price of the gift, but because they are its essence."[2]

To pontificate on their feats and foibles is their gift to us.

Notes

Preface

1. "The Naked Chief Executive," a study commissioned and published by the Government of the Isle of Man, 2008.

2. For autobiographical essays by each of these business leaders, see Venus Williams, *Come to Win: How Sports Can Help You Ace Your* Goals and Top Your Profession (New York: Amistad Press, 2012).

3. Ibid.

4. I owe this expression to MIT professor and fellow ethnographer John Van Maanen.

5. See http://gawker.com/5155015/obama-admins-sexist-sports-metaphors.

6. See http://sports.espn.go.com/espn/page2/story?page=hruby/070620.

Chapter 1

1. See L. J. Wertheim and T. Moskowitz, *Scorecasting: The Hidden Influences Behind How Sports Are Played and Games Are Won* (New York: Crown Archetype, 2011). As Wertheim and Moskowitz note, it is a rarity for a basketball team without superstars to make it to the playoffs, let alone finals. When compiling a register of the top eight basketball players, using such criteria as first-team all-stars, top-five MVP vote-getters, or even salaries,

they noticed at least one of these featured in all but one NBA finals series for the last three decades.

2. See D. Whitaker, *The Spirit of Teams* (Marlborough, UK: The Crowood Press, 1999), 12.

3. See W. C. Heinz's essay, "The Rocky Road of Pistol Pete," in *The Best American Sports Writing of the Century*, ed. David Halberstam (New York: Houghton Mifflin, 1999), 289–303, quote, 236–237.

4. Ibid.

5. See Carlo Ancelotti, *The Beautiful Games of an Ordinary Genius* (New York: Rizzolo International Publications, 2010). This quote from a prepublication online review.

6. See Walter Isaacson, "Rages, Tears and Hugs: No One Was Immune to Steve's Folly," *The Sunday Times*, 30 October 2011, 2.

7. See John Arlidge, "A World in Thrall to the iTyrant," *The Sunday Times*, October 9, 2011, 2–3.

8. See http://www.wired.com/techbiz/it/magazine/16-04/bz_apple.

9. See, for example, Joachim Stoeber, "Striving to Achieve Perfection: How Perfectionism Affects Aspirations, Emotions, and Results in Achievement Situations," working paper, The Social Life of Achievement workshop, Department of Social Anthropology, Cambridge University, September 30, 2010.

10. Teresa Amabile, "Brilliant But Cruel," *Journal of Experimental Social Psychology* 19, no. 2 (March 1983): 146–156.

11. See Rob Goffee and Gareth Jones, "Why Should Anyone Be Led by You?" *Harvard Business Review*, September 2000.

12. See Brad Darrach's wonderful essay, "The Day Bobby Blew It," in *The Best American Sports Writing of the Century*, ed. David Halberstam (New York: Houghton Mifflin, 1999), 90–128, quote, 92.

13. Ibid., 99.

14. Ibid., 243.

15. For a more elaborate description, see David Bolchover and Chris Brady, *The 90-Minute Manager* (London: Financial Times Management), 198. As the authors explain, his manager at Leeds United, Howard Wilkinson, believed that Cantona was not a team-player, omitting him from many games, and ultimately selling him to Manchester United.

16. From Jean-Philippe Leclaire and Jérôme Cazadieu, "King Eric: Ten Years On," *The Sunday Times*, May 13, 2007.

17. For a more elaborate discussion of these traits, see Daniel Gilbert, *Stumbling on Happiness* (New York: Alfred Knopf, 2006), 252–255.

18. Ed Smith, *What Sport Tells Us About Life* (London: Penguin, 2008), 29.

19. This is how Steve James described the 2010 English cricket team in *The Telegraph*, September 28, 2010, as it prepared to face Australia in the Ashes, in "The Ashes 2010: England's Boot-Camp Experience Is Just Not Cricket."

20. See Richard Rapaport's interview with Bill Walsh, "To Build a Winning Team: An Interview with Head Coach Bill Walsh," *Harvard Business Review*, January 1993. Norman Mailer's 1971 feature on Muhammad Ali is telling in this respect, too. As he wrote in *Life*: "Muhammad Ali begins with the most unsettling ego of all. Having commanded the stage, he never pretends to step back and relinquish his place to other actors—like a six-foot parrot, he keeps screaming at you that he is the center of the stage. 'Come here and get me, fool,' he says. 'You can't, 'cause you don't know who I am. You don't know *where* I am. I'm human intelligence and you don't even know if I'm good or evil.' This has been his essential message to America all these years. It is intolerable to our American mentality that the figure who is probably most prominent to us after the president is simply not comprehensible, for he could be a demon or a saint." See Norman Mailer, "Ego," in *The Best American Sports Writing of the Century*, ed. David Halberstam (New York: Houghton Mifflin, 1999), 713–737, quote, 713.

21. See *The Week* (UK ed.), October 15, 2011, 23.

22. As published in *U.S. News & World Report*, March 23, 1997, based on a poll of 1,000 Americans conducted by Market Facts. The full results are as follows: Mother Teresa (79%), Oprah Winfrey (66%), Michael Jordan (65%), Colin Powell (61%), Princess Diana (60%), Al Gore (55%), Hilary Clinton (55%), Bill Clinton (52%), Pat Robertson (47%), Newt Gingrich (40%), Dennis Rodman (28%), O. J. Simpson (19%). Survey instruments like this are blunt instruments and may need to be taken with a pinch of salt. For example, much depends on the religious views of the respondent, and the criteria he or she thinks apply when making judgments on who is, and isn't, heaven-bound. Also, the list is a predominantly Christian one. One can be forgiven for concluding that it reads much like a popularity contest.

23. The survey results are described in D. Marcum and S. Smith, *Egonomics: What Makes Our Ego Our Greatest Asset (Or Most Expensive Liability)* (New York: Simon & Schuster, 2008).

Notes

24. Steve Hollis, interview with author, May 9, 2011.

25. See, for example, Justin Kruger and David Dunning, "Unskilled and Unaware of It: How Difficulties in Recognizing One's Own Incompetence Lead to Inflated Self-assessments," *Journal of Personality and Social Psychology* 77, no. 6 (1999): 1121–1134.

26. M. A. Fuocco, "Trial and Error: They Had Larceny in Their Hearts, but Little in Their Heads," *Pittsburgh Post-Gazette*, D1, as quoted in ibid. My favorite example of stupidity in crime is Kasey G. Kazee's attempt to rob a liquor store in Ashland, Kentucky, in August 2007. In an attempt to disguise himself, he had wrapped his head in duct tape. Luckily for Kasey, it was a hot day and his sweat prevented the tape from ripping off his eyebrows when the police tore off the duct tape in an attempt to identify him.

27. From M. Diane Burton, "Rob Parson at Morgan Stanley (A)," Case 498-054 (Boston: Harvard Business School, 1998), Nasr is quoted on p. 5 of the case.

28. On matters of promotion, one of the 2010 Ig Nobel Prizes was awarded to a piece of research that, controversially, shows, by means of agent-based simulations, that not only is the Peter Principle (implying that people are promoted until they reach their maximum level of incompetence) unavoidable, but also it yields in turn a significant reduction of the global efficiency of the organization. Within a game-theory-like approach, the three authors (Alessandro Pluchino and his team at the Universitá di Catania) explored different promotion strategies and found that in order to avoid such an effect, the best ways for improving the efficiency of a given organization are either to promote an agent each time at random or to promote randomly the best and the worst members in terms of competence. So in mathematical terms, at least, it makes the most sense to promote incompetence. Sometimes.

29. Maulana wahlduddln Khan, "Depression as Blessing," *The Times of India*, May 24, 2011.

30. For more details on these traits (their benefits and risks), see Kate Ludeman and Eddie Erlandson, *Alpha Male Syndrome* (Boston: Harvard Business School Press, 2006), 12, 78.

31. Dr. Alan Bourne and Richard A. Mackinnon, "Personality and Leadership Derailment," white paper, Talent Q, info@talentq.co.uk.

32. See Ludeman and Erlandson, *Alpha Male Syndrome*, 8–9. While good estimates are hard to come by, the authors suspect 75% of top executives to be "alphas." One could argue, of course, that this high estimate reflects a typically "Western" perspective, with alpha traits being expressed differently (if at all) in societies that place a premium on collaborative problem solving, modesty, humility, and equality. And while Ludeman and Erlandson focus on alpha males, they make it clear that many of the traits attributed to these males are true of alpha females too (even if females tend to express them differently).

33. See badbossology.com for some interesting data on "bad" bosses. The survey was sponsored by Development Dimensions International.

34. The entry can be found at http://www.badbossology.com/i128879.

35. See Robert Sutton, *The No Asshole Rule* (London: Sphere, 2007), 19.

36. See S. B. Sitkin and J. R. Hackman, "Developing Team Leadership: An Interview with Coach Mike Krzyzewski," *Academy of Management Learning & Education* 10, no. 3 (2011): 494–501.

37. Alpha traits are not confined to men, of course. As Ludeman and Erlandson write, there are few differences between genders when it comes to competitiveness and drive. There do seem to be differences in the way these traits are expressed. For example, men scored higher than women on impatience and the difficulty of controlling their anger, whereas women are usually less overt. Women are emotionally more intelligent and will often prefer to seek consensus. Their ability to empathize and be sensitive to the feelings of others can pay dividends but could be ineffective when dealing with those who need a more direct approach. And conflict avoidance can suppress internal competition, or drive it underground, and clear the air by exchanging strongly held points of view. So it seems one cannot have one's cake and eat it too.

38. Steve James, "The Ashes 2010: England's Boot Camp Experience Is Just Not Cricket," *The Telegraph*, October 28, 2010.

39. Ibid.

40. Nick Hoult, "The Ashes 2010: England's Secret Bonding Trip Was Beneficial, Says Andrew Strauss," *The Telegraph*, October 28, 2010.

41. Andy Wilson, "England's 'Boot Camp' Called into Question After James Anderson Injury," *Guardian*, October 15, 2010.

42. Martin Samuels in *The Times* as reprinted in *The Week*, November 10, 2007, 10.

43. See Michael W. Kraus, Cassy Huang, and Dacher Keltner, "Tactile Communication, Cooperation, and Performance: An Ethological Study of the NBA," working paper, University of California–Berkeley, 2010.

44. Julian Andrews, *What It Takes to Earn Your Place* (London: Third Millennium Publishing, Ltd., 2004), 12.

Chapter 2

1. See John Kay, "Football's Example Can Help Companies Score," *Financial Times*, July 11, 2006.

2. See Marina Hyde, "On This Evidence 'Plucky Slovenia' Will Hand England Their Backsides," *Guardian* online, June 18, 2010, http://www.guardian.co.uk/football/blog/2010/jun/18/world-cup-2010-england-algeria1.

3. See, for example, user-contributed commentaries at http://everything2.com/title/2004+U.S.+Olympic+Men%2527s+Basketball+Team.

4. Data on final standings is available on Wikipedia. The example came from G. Colvin, *Talent Is Overrated: What Really Separates World-Class Performers from Everybody Else* (London: Nicholas Brealey, 2008), 136.

5. Mark Richardson, interview with author, February 28, 2011.

6. As quoted in D. Bolchover and C. Brady, *The 90-Minute Manager: Lessons from the Sharp End of Management* (Harlow, UK: Pearson Education Ltd., 2004/2002), 207.

7. Ibid., 207.

8. David Hemery, 1968 Olympic gold medalist in the 400-meter hurdles, interview with author, March 19, 2011.

9. See L. K. Kahn, "The Sports Business as a Labor Market Laboratory," *Journal of Economic Perspectives* 14, no. 3 (2000): 75–76. Kahn's estimate for the average wage of full-time, full-year equivalent workers is based on data provided by the U.S. Bureau of Labor Statistics, 1998.

10. See Stefan Szymanski, "Income Inequality, Competitive Balance and the Attractiveness of Team Sports: Some Evidence and a Natural Experiment from English Soccer," *The Economic Journal*, 2001.

11. See Michael Lewis, *Moneyball: The Art of Winning an Unfair Game* (New York: W.W. Norton & Co, 2003). The Oakland A's were able to

achieve this by the application of statistics to game results, allowing them to identify, and buy, undervalued players. The specific case of the Oakland A's is discussed in more detail in chapter 7.

12. These findings are controversial in that they counter prior research. For a discussion of their sample, method, and results see S. A. Dennis, S. L. Nelson, and N. Beneda, "Player Salaries and Team Performance in Major League Baseball," *Review of Business Research* 9, no. 4 (2009): 174–182.

13. See P. M. Sommers, "Work Incentives and Salary Distributions in the National Hockey League," *Atlantic Economic Journal* 26, no. 1 (1998): 119, as cited in D. J. Berri and R. T. Jewell, "Wage Inequality and Firm Performance: Professional Basketball's Natural Experiment," *Atlantic Economic Journal* 32, no. 2 (2004): 130–139.

14. See Berri and Jewell, "Wage Inequality and Firm Performance."

15. See, for example, Milgrom and Roberts, 1988; Akerlof and Yellen, 1988; Akerlof and Yellen, 1990; Levine, 1991; Lazear, 1989 and 1991, as cited in Berri and Jewell, "Wage Inequality and Firm Performance."

16. See, for example, the work of Ramaswamy and Rowthorn, 1991; Lazear and Rosen, 1981; and Rosen, 1986, all as cited in Berri and Jewell, "Wage Inequality and Firm Performance."

17. See B. Groysberg, J. T. Polzer, and H. A. Elfenbein, "Too Many Cooks Spoil the Broth: How High Status Individuals Decrease Group Effectiveness," *Organization Science* 22, no. 3 (May/June 2011): 722–737. See also, "The Diminishing Returns of All-Star Teams," *Strategy+Business*, http://www.strategy-business.com/article/re00112?gko=018a4.

18. See Miguel Helft, "Big Tech Firms Pay Top Dollar for Start-ups, When They Just Want the Bodies," *International Herald Tribune*, May 19, 2011, 15.

19. See "The Catalan Kings,'" *The Economist*, March 19, 2011, http://www.economist.com/node/18709691.

20. See P. Jackson, *Sacred Hoops: Spiritual Lessons of a Hardwood Warrior* (New York: Hyperion, 2006), 19.

21. See B. Groysberg, L.-E. Lee and R. Abrahams, "What It Takes to Make 'Star' Hires Pay Off," *MIT Sloan Management Review* 51, no. 2 (2010): 57–61.

22. See Kate Ludeman and Eddie Erlandson, *Alpha Male Syndrome* (Boston: Harvard Business School Press, 2006).

23. See Jackson, *Sacred Hoops*, 5.

24. Ron Dennis, interview, Mail Online March 15, 2011, http://www.dailymail.co.uk/home/moslive/article-1355918/Ron-Dennis-If-dont-bleed-McLaren-youre-wrong-company.html.

25. Matt Guinness-King, interview, *The Cambridge Student*, March 3, 2011.

26. See T. Casciaro and M. Sousa Lobo, "Competent Jerks, Lovable Fools, and the Formation of Social Networks," *Harvard Business Review*, June 2005.

27. Author interview with Steve Hollis.

28. See J. Groopman, *How Doctors Think* (New York: First Mariner Books, 2007), for references to Judy Hall and Debra Roter's extensive body of research. See also J. Hall and D. Roter, *Doctors Talking with Patients/Patients Talking with Doctors: Improving Communication in Medical Visits*, 2nd ed. (Westport, CT: Praeger Publishers, 2006).

29. Bobby Thatcher's story is told in great detail in J. Raymond, "Memoir: The One That Got Away," *Prospect,* 2011, http://www.prospectmagazine.co.uk/tag/rowing-boat/. It is also available in e-book form as *Race of Spears: The Art of Rowing* (Battle, UK: Ether Books Ltd., 2011).

30. Ibid.

31. See Peter Gammons, ed., *The Best American Sports Writing 2010* (London: Houghton Mifflin Harcourt, 2010), 255–256.

32. See Mark de Rond, "Lessons from the Oxford and Cambridge Boat Race," *Harvard Business Review,* September 2008.

Chapter 3

1. Magic Johnson and Larry Bird are quoted in a nice study of rivalry in basketball. See G. J. Kilduff, H. A. Elfenbein, and B. M. Staw, "The Psychology of Rivalry: A Relationally-Dependent Analysis of Competition," *Academy of Management Journal* 53, no. 5, 943–969.

2. See National Basketball Association, *The Perfect Team: The Best Players, Coach and GM—Let the Debate Begin!* (New York: Doubleday, 2006).

3. Ibid., 85.

4. See Jack Denfeld Wood, "New Haven Nighthawks," in *Groups That Work and Those That Don't: Creating Conditions for Effective Teamwork*, ed. R. Hackman (San Francisco: Jossey-Bass, 1989).

Notes

5. M. de Rond, *The Last Amateurs: To Hell and Back with the Cambridge Boat Race Crew* (London: ICON Books, 2008), 107.

6. Jake used to spend long hours at my house during this period in early 2007. This excerpt was taken from my ethnographic study of the Cambridge University Boat Club during 2006–2007. As an ethnographer, I "lived with" the squad full-time for 199 days as they trained and prepared to select a crew to race Oxford. The results of this study were reported in de Rond, *The Last Amateurs.*

7. See W. T. Gallwey, *The Inner Game of Tennis* (London: Pan Books, 1975, 1986), 111.

8. See Nancy Katz, "Sports Teams as a Model for Workplace Teams: Lessons and Liabilities," *Academy of Management Executive* 15, no. 3 (2001): 56–69.

9. See R. Hackman, *Collaborative Intelligence: Using Teams to Solve Hard Problems* (San Francisco: Berrett-Koehler Publishers, 2011), 13.

10. Richard Hackman is quoted in Ross's article. See Judith A. Ross, "Team Camaraderie: Can You Have Too Much?" *Harvard Management Update,* November 2005, http://blogs.hbr.org/hmu/2008/02/team-camaraderie-can-you-have-1.html.

11. See R. Hackman, "Why Teams Don't Work," *Harvard Business Review,* May 2009, 98–105.

12. See D. Goleman, "Leading Resonant Teams," in *Leader to Leader: Enduring Insights on Leadership 2,* eds. F. Hesselbein and A. Shrader (San Francisco: Jossey-Bass, 2008), 186–195.

13. See Hackman, *Collaborative Intelligence,* 13.

14. Richard Hackman cites several reviews, including R. Hackman and R. Wageman, "A Theory of Team Coaching," *Academy of Management Review* 30 (2005): 269–287; R. E. Kaplan, "The Utility of Maintaining Work Relationships Openly: An Experimental Study," *Journal of Applied Behavioral Science* 15 (1979): 41–59; R. W. Woodman and J. J. Sherwood, "The Role of Team Development in Organizational Effectiveness: A Critical Review," *Psychological Bulletin* 88 (1980): 166–186; and A. W. Woolley, "Effects of Intervention Content and Timing on Group Task Performance," *Journal of Applied Behavioral Science* 34 (1998): 30–49. All are cited in Hackman, *Collaborative Intelligence,* 13.

15. For the original article, see B. M. Staw, "Attribution of the 'Causes' of Performance: A General Alternative Interpretation of Cross-sectional

Research on Organizations," *Organizational Behavior and Human Performance* 13, no. 3 (1975): 414–432.

16. See Richard Rapaport, "To Build a Winning Team: An Interview with Head Coach Bill Walsh," *Harvard Business Review*, Jan 1, 1993.

17. As quoted in D. Bolchover and C. Brady, *The 90-Minute Manager: Lessons from the Sharp End of Management* (Harlow, UK: Pearson Education Ltd., 2004, 2002), 208.

18. Ibid., 208.

19. See D. Halberstam, *The Amateurs* (New York: Random House, 1985), 44.

20. See S. Snook and J. T. Polzer, "The Army Crew Team," Case 9-403-131 (Boston: Harvard Business School, 2003). The accompanying Teaching Note (5-404-117) details the coach's solution.

21. Ibid.

22. See B. M. Staw and H. Hoang, "Sunk costs in the NBA: Why Draft Order Affects Playing Time and Survival in Professional Basketball," *Administrative Science Quarterly* 40 (1995): 474–494.

23. See M. Lewis, "The No-Stats All-Star," in *The Best American Sports Writing 2010*, ed. Peter Gammons (London: Houghton Mifflin Harcourt, 2010), 254.

24. Interview by author.

25. See A. Field, "Are You Rewarding Solo Performance at the Team's Expense?" in *Managing Teams for High Performance* (Boston: Harvard Business School Press, 2007), 17–19.

26. The Sony, DaimlerChrysler, and Microsoft examples are from Herminia Ibarra and Morten T. Hansen, "Getting Collaboration Right," HBR blog, May 16, 2011.

27. See K. Merriman, "Low-trust Teams Prefer Individualized Pay," *Harvard Business Review*, November 2008.

28. See K. T. Dirks, "Trust in Leadership and Team Performance: Evidence from NCAA Basketball," *Journal of Applied Psychology* 85, no. 6 (2000): 1004–1012.

29. See F. Bidault and A. Castello, "Why Too Much Trust is Death to Innovation," *MIT Sloan Management Review*, May 10, 2010.

30. See C. W. Langfred, "Too Much of a Good Thing? Negative Effects of High Trust and Individual Autonomy in Self-managed Teams," *Academy of Management Journal* 47, no. 3 (2004): 385–399.

31. See B. L. Kirkman and B. Rosen, "Beyond Self-management: Antecedents and Consequences of Team Empowerment," *Academy of Management Journal* 42, no. 1 (1999): 58–74.

32. See Bolchover and Brady, *The 90-Minute Manager*, 194.

33. Ibid., 195.

34. As quoted in "Ferguson Shares Recipe for Success: Philosophy, History and Mentality," *The Independent*, April 30, 2011, Sports, 2.

35. See R. Hackman and N. Katz, "Group Behavior and Performance," in *Handbook of Social Psychology*, 5th ed., eds. S. T. Fiske, D. T. Gilbert and G. Lindzey (New York: Wiley, 2010), 1208–1251. The extended study is reported in H. C. Foushee, J. K. Lauber, M. M. Baetge, and D. B. Acomb, "Crew Factors in Flight Operations: III. The Operational Significance of Exposure to Short-haul Air Transport Operations," Technical Memorandum No. 88342 (Moffett Field, CA: NASA Ames Research Center, 1986).

36. See C. D. Parks and A. B. Stone, "The Desire to Expel Unselfish Members from the Group," *Journal of Personality and Social Psychology* 99, no. 2 (2010): 303–310. The study's findings were reported in *The Economist*, August 19, 2010, http://www.economist.com/node/16843817?story_id= 16843817), and on http://blogs.hbr.org/cs/2010/09/when_selfless_ behavior_in_a_gr.html.

37. See D. Ernst and J. Bamford, "Your Alliances Are Too Stable," *Harvard Business Review*, June 2005, 8.

Chapter 4

1. See Brad Darrach's essay, "The Day Bobby Blew It," in *The Best American Sports Writing of the Century*, ed. D. Halberstam (New York: Houghton Mifflin, 1999), 90–128.

2. M. de Rond, *The Last Amateurs: To Hell and Back with the Cambridge Boat Race Crew* (London: ICON Books, 2008), 186.

3. See E. Smith, *What Sport Tells Us About Life* (London: Penguin, 2008).

4. Ibid., 67.

5. Ibid., 73.

6. Duncan Fletcher's version of Michael Vaughan's play is detailed in Ed Smith's chapter, "Why History Matters," in his *What Sport Tells Us About Life*, 76–78.

Notes

7. See http://stevehacking.blogspot.com/2009_10_01_archive.html. Steve Hacking is a professional rugby player, former McKinsey consultant, and founding partner of Latitude.

8. See J. Runde and M. de Rond, "Evaluating Causal Explanation of Specific Events," *Organization Studies* 31, no. 4 (April 2010): 431–450.

9. Sixty-seven percent of the 285,000 motorcycles that Honda produced in 1959 were Super Cubs.

10. Honda executive Kihachiro Kawashima, quoted in R. Pascale, "The 'Honda Effect' Revisited," *California Management Review* 38 (1996): 78–117.

11. See R. Rumelt, "The 'Honda Effect' Revisited," *California Management Review* 38 (1996): 78–117.

12. See J. Kay, "Relativism Rules," *Financial Times*, February 21, 2001, johnkay.com.

13. See M. Goold, "The 'Honda Effect' Revisited," *California Management Review* 38 (1996): 78–117.

14. R. T. Pascale and G. A. Athos, *The Art of Japanese Management* (London: Penguin Books Ltd, 1986).

15. R. Pascale, "Zen and the Art of Management," *Harvard Business Review* 56, no. 2 (1978): 153–162.

16. Henry Mintzberg, *The Nature of Managerial Work* (New York: Harper & Row, 1973), iv.

17. See A. King and M. de Rond, "Boat Race: Rhythm and the Possibility of Collective Performance," *British Journal of Sociology* 62, no. 4 (2011): 565–585.

18. Adrian Moorhouse, interview with author, February 28, 2011. The manager's name is a pseudonym.

19. The GROW model is relatively well known. The model on which I rely (and which I've slightly adapted) is that used by David Whittaker and David Hemery.

Chapter 5

1. A bit of trivia from the British television program *QI*, hosted by Stephen Fry.

2. See Sian Griffiths, "The Canadian Who Invented Basketball," *BBC Sport*, http://www.bbc.co.uk/news/world-us-canada-11348053.

Notes

3. See Eli Saslow, "The Old Ba' Game," in *The Best American Sports Writing,* ed. William Nack (New York: Houghton Mifflin Company, 2008), 212–219.

4. See "History of Football," *Encyclopedia of British Football,* http://www.spartacus.schoolnet.co.uk/Fhistory.htm.

5. See "More Scientists Treat Experiments as a Team Sport," *Wall Street Journal,* November 23, 2009, http://online.wsj.com/article/SB125868444693956911.html.

6. D. Kavitz and B. Martin, "Ringelmann Rediscovered: The Original Article," *Journal of Personality and Social Psychology* 50, no 5 (1986): 936–941. Ringelmann's original articles include: M. Ringelmann, *Recherches sur les moteurs animals: Essais des boeufs de travail* ["Research on animate sources of power: Tests of oxen"], *Annales de l'Institut National Agronomique, 2e serie—tome VI (1907):* 243–279; M. Ringelmann, *Appareils de culture mecanique avec treuils et cables (resultats d'essais)* ["Mechanical tilling equipment with winches and cables (results of tests)"], *Annales de l'Institut National Agronomique, 2e ss XII (1913a):* 299–343; M. Ringelmann, *Recherches sur les moteurs animals: Travail de l'homme* ["Research on animate sources of power: The work of man"], *Annales de l'Institut National Agronomique, 2e serie—tome XII (1913b):* 1–40.

7. A. G. Ingham, G. Levinger, J. Graves, and V. Peckham, "The Ringelmann Effect: Studies of Group Size and Group Performance," *Journal of Experimental Social Psychology* 10 (1974): 371–384.

8. See http://www.bbc.co.uk/news/magazine-15265317.

9. For a review of various social loafing studies, see S. J. Karau and K. D. Williams, "Social Loafing: a Meta-analytic Review and Theoretical Implications," *Journal of Personality and Social Psychology* 65, no. 4 (1993): 681–706.

10. For references on various experiments on social loafing please refer to an excellent review by Leslie A. DeChurch and Jessica R. Mesmer-Magnus, "The Cognitive Underpinnings of Effective Teamwork: A Meta-Analysis," *Journal of Applied Psychology* 95, no. 1 (2010): 32–53.

11. J. R. Hackman and N. Vidmar, "Effects of Size and Task Type on Group Performance and Member Reaction," *Sociometry* 33 (1970): 37–54. For details on this and related studies, see also J. R. Hackman, *Leading Teams: Setting the Stage for Great Performances* (Boston: Harvard Business School Press, 2002), 118–119. The optimal team size, according to Hackman and Vidmar is 4.6.

Notes

12. See J. A. Myers and R. E. Norris, *Summary of Results: B-737 Crew Complement Evaluation* (Elk Grove Village, IL: United Airlines, 1968), as cited in Hackman, *Leading Teams*, 118–119.

13. The next three examples are reported in "Team Performance and Team Size," Team Building, http://ezinearticles.com/?Creativity-Management-and-Team-Size&id=63030.

14. See "More People, More Bugs," Projects@Work, October 6, 2005, http://www.projectsatwork.com/content/articles/227526.cfm. See also Quantitative Software Management at http://www.qsm.com/.

15. J. R. Katzenbach and D. K. Smith, *The Wisdom of Teams* (New York: Harper Business, 2003).

16. See Kal Bishop, "Creativity Management and Team Size," Ezine articles, http://ezinearticles.com/?Creativity-Management-and-Team-Size&id=63030.

17. "War for Talent, Part Two," a 2008 update on McKinsey's original 1997 survey called "War for Talent: Organization and Leadership Practice," published by McKinsey & Company, 2001.

18. In an attempt to mimic the fast-feedback culture of sports in retail outlets, Nick Wilkinson at Currys & Dixons used a real-time electronic system that not only measured sales performance by the hour but provided an instant comparison to performance that same hour twelve months earlier. Eager to curb the habit of blaming poor performance on the weather or competition rather than lack of collective effort, this system helped generate a far greater awareness of accountability and ownership within individual stores.

19. Parts of the dialogue in this paragraph are taken verbatim from the film, *The Abilene Paradox*, narrated by Jerry Harvey. The film can be purchased at www.abileneparadox.com.

20. For a more detailed discussion of the Abilene paradox, see W. G. Dyer, W. G. Dyer Jr., and J. H. Dyer, *Team Building: Proves Strategies for Improving Team Performance*, 4th ed. (San Francisco: Jossey-Bass, 2007), ch. 8.

21. P. F. Drucker, "Managing for Business Effectiveness," *Harvard Business Review*, May 1963.

22. For the full story, see M. de Rond, *The Last Amateurs: To Hell and Back with the Cambridge Boat Race Crew* (London: ICON Books, 2008).

23. A. E. Edmondson, "Learning from Mistakes Is Easier Said Than Done: Group and Organizational Influences on the Detection and Correction of Human Error," *Journal of Applied Behavioral Science* 32 (1996):

5–28, as cited in Hackman, *Leading Teams*. See also J. R. Hackman, "Learning More by Crossing Levels: Evidence from Airplanes, Hospitals, and Orchestras," *Journal of Organizational Behavior* 24 (2003): 905–922.

24. See A. Edmondson, R. Bohmer, and G. Pisano, "Speeding Up Team Learning," *Harvard Business Review*, October 2001.

25. See, for example, G. Stasser, S. I. Vaughan, and D. D. Stewart, "Pooling Unshared Information: The Benefits of Knowing How Access to Information Is Distributed Among Group Members," *Organizational Behavior and Human Decision Processes* 82, no. 1 (2000): 102–116.

26. Study is cited in R. B. Cialdini, "How to Get the Best Solutions from Your Team," in *Managing Teams for High Performance* (Boston: Harvard Business School Press, 2007), 46–49.

27. See J. D. Westphal and M. K. Bednar, "Pluralistic Ignorance in Corporate Boards and Firms' Strategic Persistence in Response to Low Firm Performance," *Administrative Science Quarterly* 50, no. 2 (2005): 262–298. This article is mentioned in Freek Vermeulen's provocative, *Business Exposed: The Naked Truth About What Really Goes On in the World of Business* (London: Prentice Hall, 2010), in conjunction with the Abilene paradox.

28. Some of these suggestions originate from the teaching notes to an excellent, computer-aided, team-based exercise, "Everest," available from Harvard Business School Publishing.

Chapter 6

1. Adrian Moorhouse, interview with author, February 28, 2011.

2. The Jamaican Usain Bolt holds the record (at the time of writing) of 9.58 seconds; Leroy Burrell, Justin Gatlin, and Olusoji Fasuba share eighth place with a time of 9.85 seconds. See http://en.wikipedia.org/wiki/100_metres.

3. Though this odd result is sometimes attributed to the finish-line umpire falling asleep, it is worth remembering that there was no defined finish line in 1877. As one boat race historian points out, "the crush of craft around the finish was such that the skiff of the judge may well have been substantially out of position. This was rectified in 1878 when the finish was marked by a post." For details, see the official Boat Race Web site, www. theboatrace.org.

4. See http://www.motorsportsetc.com/info/f1_mrgns.htm.

5. See http://en.espnf1.com/f1/motorsport/story/31712.html.

6. See M. Gladwell, *Outliers: The Story of Success* (New York: Little, Brown, 2008), 22–23.

7. In fact, it would be interesting to see whether Gladwell's popularization of the importance of birth date for Canadian ice hockey players has had any effect on subsequent births (meaning there are now even more births recorded in the first few months of the year as compared with other months) or on setting cutoff dates for junior hockey leagues.

8. See J. Apesteguia and I. Palacios-Huerta, "Psychological Pressure in Competitive Environments: Evidence from a Randomized Natural Experiment," *American Economic Review* 100 (December 2010): 2548–2564.

9. Ibid.

10. See Russell Adam, "Baseball Confronts the Luck Factor," *Wall Street Journal*, June 24, 2006, http://online.wsj.com/article/SB115109391791589205.html.

11. As quoted in Seve Ballesteros, obituary, *The Week*, 817, May 14, 2011, 38.

12. See http://sweatscience.com/do-sports-superstitions-really-work/.

13. See Piercarlo Valdesolo, "Why 'Magical Thinking' Works for Some People," http://www.scientificamerican.com/article.cfm?id=superstitions-can-make-you.

14. See http://www.mmamania.com/2009/03/23/lyoto-machida-drinks-his-own-urine-every-morning/.

15. See L. Block and T. Kramer, "The Effect of Superstitious Beliefs on Performance Expectations," *Journal of the Academy of Marketing Science* 37, no. 3 (2009): 161–169.

16. See S. Makridakis, R. Hogarth, and A. Gaba, *Dance with Chance: Making Luck Work for You* (Oxford, UK: Oneworld Publications, 2009), x.

17. Arguably this might have prevented the spread of head lice, meaning the superstition had merits beyond an allusion of control. Interestingly, in 1948, B. F. Skinner, a behavioral psychologist, published an article in the *Journal of Experimental Psychology*, in which he described his pigeons exhibiting what appeared to be superstitious behavior: a pigeon turning in its cage or swinging its head in a pendulum motion. Skinner argued that, because these behaviors were all done ritualistically in an attempt to receive food from a dispenser, even though the dispenser had already been programmed to release food at set time intervals regardless of the pigeons' actions, pigeons

were trying to influence their feeding schedule by performing these actions. He then extended this as a proposition regarding the nature of superstitious behavior in humans, see http://en.wikipedia.org/ wiki/B_f_skinner.

18. Salt used to be a precious commodity. In fact, Roman soldiers were paid in salt, hence the world *salary*. To throw salt over one's left shoulder means to throw it into the eyes of the devil (who, some argue, stands behind it).

19. There are sound reasons for some superstitions. To not clip one's nails at night hails back to the days before electricity became commonplace and may have simply served to protect people from injury. A similar reasoning applies to not sweeping the floor after sunset because dropped valuables might inadvertently get lost forever. For an interesting discussion on these and other superstitions, see http://www.gurjari.net/ico/Mystica/html/popular_superstitions.htm.

20. See B. Malinowski, *Magic, Science and Religion and Other Essays* (Garden City, NY: Doubleday, 1954). See Jared L. Bleak and Christina M. Frederick, "Superstitious Behavior in Sport: Levels of Effectiveness and Determinants of Use in three Collegiate Sports," *Journal of Sport Behavior* 21 (1998).

21. See M. Womack, "Why Athletes Need Ritual: A Study of Magic Among Professional Athletes," in Shirl Hoffman (ed.), *Sport and Religion* (Champaign, IL: Human Kinetics, 1992), 191–202.

22. H. Buhrmann and M. Zaugg, "Superstitions Among Basketball Players," *Journal of Sports Behavior* 4, no. 4 (1981): 163–174.

23. See G. Neil, B. Anderson, and W. Sheppard, "Superstitions Among Male and Female Athletes of Various Levels of Involvement," *Journal of Sport Behavior* 4, no. 3 (1981): 137–148.

24. See J. L. Van-Raalte, B. W. Brewer, C. J. Nemeroff, and D. E. Linder, "Chance Orientation and Superstitious Behavior on the Putting Green," *Journal of Sports Behavior* 14, no. 1 (1991): 41–50.

25. See C. J. Gregory and B. M. Petrie, "Superstitions of Canadian Intercollegiate Athletes: An Inter-Sport Comparison," *International Review for the Sociology of Sports* 10, no. 2 (1975): 59–68.

26. See L. Damisch, B. Stoberock, and T. Mussweiler, "Keep Your Fingers Crossed! How Superstition Improves Performance," *Psychological Science* 21, no. 7 (2010): 1014–1020.

27. The German equivalent of "keeping fingers crossed" is "keeping thumbs pressed." The two control groups were given a similar—but not superstitious—instruction.

28. The students were led to believe that these performance tests were entirely unrelated to a survey on lucky charms. Anyone who guessed the connection would have been excluded from the results.

29. See Valdesolo, "Why 'Magical Thinking' Works for Some People."

30. See Jennifer Wang, "Turn Superstition into Marketing Gold," *Entrepreneur*, February 11, 2009, http://www.entrepreneur.com/article/200024.

31. The theory claims the stock market will rise if a National Football Conference team wins the game. Likewise, if an American Football Conference team wins, the market will drop. The indicator was correct 25 times in 37 years from 1967 through 2003, an almost 68% success rate. For details, see: http://www.investinganswers.com/a/four-wall-street-superstitions-just-wont-die-1905.

32. See G. M. Lepori, "Dark Omens in the Sky: Do Superstitious Beliefs Affect Investment Decisions?" working paper, Copenhagen Business School. For a discussion of the original article, see http://www.economist.com/node/14081809.

33. See http://www.beursgorilla.nl/jacko.asp.

34. See J. M. Campanario, "Using Citation Classics to Study the Incidence of Serendipity in Scientific Discovery," *Scientometrics* 37 (1996): 3–24.

35. See M. de Rond and I. Morley, eds., *Serendipity: Fortune and the Prepared Mind* (Cambridge, UK: Cambridge University Press, 2010).

36. See G. Jones and A. Moorhouse, *Developing Mental Toughness: Gold Medal Strategies for Transforming Your Business Performance* (Oxford, UK: Spring Hill, 2008), 12. The original quote is found in David Beckham, *My Side* (London: Collins Willow, 2003), 273–274.

37. Jones and Moorhouse, *Developing Mental Toughness,* 26–27.

38. Ibid., 81.

39. Ibid., 79.

40. Interview with author.

41. The term "impostor syndrome" was first coined by Pauline R. Clance and Suzanne A. Imes, "The Imposter Phenomenon Among High

Achieving Women: Dynamics and Therapeutic Intervention," *Psychotherapy Theory, Research and Practice* 15, no. 3 (1978): 241–247.

42. According to Valerie Young, on the impostor syndrome. For details on her work and a series of insightful articles, see http://impostorsyndrome.com/InformationAndArticles.pdf.

43. For a discussion on the impostor syndrome in business, see http://www.impostorsyndrome.com/press/executivefemale031986.htm.

Chapter 7

1. See Kathryn Schulz's insightful review: "Michael Lewis and *Moneyball*: Being Wrong About Sports," http://beingwrongbook.com/blog/michael-lewis-and-moneyball-being-wrong-about-sports, March 12, 2010.

2. M. Lewis, *Moneyball: The Art of Winning an Unfair Game* (London: W. W. Norton & Co., 2003).

3. See Brian O'Neill's book review of *Moneyball* in the *Pittsburgh Post Gazette*, May 25, 2003.

4. Its name comes from the abbreviation SABR, which stands for the Society for American Baseball Research. Sabermetrics has gained momentum in recent years for several reasons: new advances in ball tracking that provide more data from which to build more powerful statistics, and the general success of teams that adhere to sabermetric principles. In many ways, sabermetrics exists on the opposite end of the spectrum from scouting, and arguments often fall along the lines of traditional scouts, usually ex-players, versus young academics and statisticians. One reason for the tension between these old and new schools of baseball thought is that sabermetric conclusions often challenge conventional wisdom.

5. For more details, see James Albert, "An Introduction to Sabermetrics," Bowling Green State University, http://www-math.bgsu.edu/~albert/papers/saber.htm.

6. See Alan Schwartz, "The Mazzone Touch Is More Than Just Perception," *New York Times*, May 22, 2005, http://www.nytimes.com/2005/05/22/sports/baseball/22score.html.

7. See J. Thorn and P. Palmer, *Total Baseball* (New York: Harper Collins, 1993).

8. See J. C. Bradbury, *The Baseball Economist: The Real Game Exposed* (London: Plume, 2008).

9. See Jacob Silverman, "How Sabermetrics Works," http://entertainment. howstuffworks.com/sabermetrics4.htm.

10. See Schwartz, "The Mazzone Touch Is More Than Just Perception."

11. See S. C. Albright, "A Statistical Analysis of Hitting Streaks in Baseball," *Journal of the American Statistical Association* 88 (1993): 1175–1183.

12. See T. J. Moskowitz and L. J. Wertheim, *Scorecasting: The Hidden Influences Behind How Sports Are Played and Games Are Won* (New York: Crown Archetype, 2011), 215–229.

13. Ibid., 221.

14. Ibid., 221.

15. The five players (according to one of *Moneyball*'s critics) are: Carlos Peña, Prince Fielder, Scott Kazmir, Zack Greinke, and Jeremy Bonderman.

16. See M. Lewis, "The No-Stats All-Star," in *The Best American Sports Writing 2010*, ed. Peter Gammons (London: Houghton Mifflin Harcourt, 2010), 252.

17. Ibid., 253.

18. As quoted in an article by Stephen Jones, "Hi-tech Heroes Show True Heart," *Sunday Times*, November 14, 2010, 3.

19. T. H. Davenport, "Competing on Analytics," *Harvard Business Review*, January 2006, 98–107.

20. Through his New England Sports Venture.

21. See Duncan White, "Liverpool Owners Looking to Use Baseball Principles of Statistical Analysis," *The Telegraph*, February 1, 2011, http://www.telegraph.co.uk/sport/football/teams/liverpool/8098829/Liverpool-owners-looking-to-use-baseball-principles-such-as-Moneyball-and-Sabermetrics.html.

22. See BBC correspondent Phil McNulty's blog, "Torres and Carroll Lead Frenzy," http://www.bbc.co.uk/blogs/philmcnulty/2011/02/if_januarys_transfer_deadline.html.

23. See T. H. Davenport and J. G. Harris, *Competing on Analytics: The New Science of Winning* (Boston: Harvard Business School Press, 2007).

24. See F. W. Taylor, *The Principles of Scientific Management* (Seattle: CreateSpace [an Amazon company], 2011, originally published in 1911]).

25. For example, Walmart's database is estimated at 600 terabytes. See http://www.bestpricecomputers.co.uk/glossary/business_analytics.htm.

26. See R. Kohavi, N. J. Rothleder, and E. Simoudis, "Emerging Trends in Business Analysis," *Communications of the ACM* 45, no. 8 (2002): 45–48.

27. As quoted by Davenport and Harris in *Competing on Analytics*, 26. The original source can be found in Pat Curry, "The Future of FICO," Bankrate.com, November 1, 2005.

28. So successful was the experiment that Signet decided to spin off Capital One as a separate company. While a nice example of exploiting data to target more profitable markets, Capital One's approach has since been described as predatory, and, in November 2008, its exposure to subprime customers necessitated a $3.56 billion bailout by the Emergency Economic Stabilization Act. See Davenport and Harris, *Competing on Analytics*, 41–42.

29. He referred to these as mechanical methods of prediction by combining the results of various tests.

30. See B. Kleinmuntz, "Why We Still Use Our Heads Instead of Formulas: Toward an Integrative Approach," *Psychological Bulletin* 107, no. 3 (1990): 296–310.

31. See P. E. Meehl, *Clinical Versus Statistical Prediction: A Theoretical Analysis and Review of the Evidence* (Minneapolis, MN: Jason Aronson Inc., 1996, originally published 1954).

32. See Kleinmuntz, "Why We Still Use Our Heads Instead of Formulas," 297.

33. P. E. Meehl, "Causes and Effects of My Disturbing Little Book," *Journal of Personality Assessment* 50 (1986): 370–375.

34. See Michael Schrage, "Moneyball, Geeks and the New Era of Human Performance Analytics," *Harvard Business Review* blog, http://blogs.hbr.org/schrage/2010/03/moneyball-geeks-and-the-new-er.html.

35. Ibid.

36. See G. Anders, *The Rare Find: Spotting Exceptional Talent Before Everyone Else* (London: Penguin, 2011), 28.

37. Ibid., 115–116.

38. Ibid., 243.

39. Malcolm Gladwell's *Blink* has been subject to various criticisms, one of the more significant which is entailed in Michael LeGault, *Think!: Why*

Crucial Decisions Can't Be Made in the Blink of an Eye (New York: Simon and Schuster, 2006).

40. See H. J. Einhorn, "Expert Measurement and Mechanical Combination," *Organizational Behavior and Human Performance* 7 (1972): 86–106, as cited in Kleinmuntz, "Why We Still Use Our Heads Instead of Formulas," 301.

41. R. C. Blattberg and S. J. Hoch, "Database Models and Managerial Intuition: 50% Model + 50% Manager," *Management Science,* as cited in Kleinmuntz, "Why We Still Use Our Heads Instead of Formulas," 301.

Conclusion

1. See James March and Thierry Weil, *On Leadership: A Short Course* (Oxford, UK: Wiley-Blackwell, 2005).

2. See David Foster Wallace, "How Tracy Austin Broke My Heart," in *Consider the Lobster, and Other Essays* (New York: Little, Brown, 2006), 155.

Index

Index

Index

Index

About the Author

MARK DE ROND is on the faculty of Judge Business School at the University of Cambridge. He completed his doctorate at Oxford University and later studied negotiation skills and conflict resolution at the Program on Negotiation at Harvard Law School. Mark was a visiting scholar at the Wharton School in 2001 and a Fulbright Distinguished Scholar at Stanford University in 2008.

He is an experienced and popular teacher, including with major blue-chip companies, government offices, and nonprofit organizations where he runs workshops. His publications include two award-winning articles and two books on strategic alliances. His first book, *Strategic Alliances as Social Facts: Business, Biotechnology, and Intellectual History,* received the 2005 George R. Terry Book Award from the Academy of Management, awarded annually to the book judged to have made the most significant contribution to advancing management knowledge.

Mark's fieldwork as an ethnographer with the Cambridge University Boat Club was the subject of his second book: *The Last Amateurs: To Hell and Back with the Cambridge Boat Race Crew.* Elements of this research have been featured in *Time* magazine,

About the Author

The Economist, the *Financial Times,* the *Times* (London), the *Week,* the *Independent,* the *Telegraph,* and the *Guardian,* as well as on the BBC. The book was selected by the *Financial Times* as one of twelve Best Business Books of 2008 and by *BBC Sport* as one of ten Best Sporting Reads of 2008. It was a top ten book on J. P. Morgan's 2009 Summer Reading list and won Mark the 2009 Imagination Lab Award, given to one academic each year for scholarship that is both innovative and rigorous.

Mark conducts research the old-fashioned way: by embedding himself with teams full-time. His latest two-year project involved a stint with military surgeons in Afghanistan's Helmand province in 2011.